The Pain I F

The Children of Israel

7th October and Beyond -

An Islamic Perspective

Dr Mohammed Fahim PhD

أَعـوذُ بِاللهِ مِنَ الشَّيْطانِ الرَّجيـم

I seek refuge in God, from Satan, the accursed
one

سورة النمل
Surah An-Naml (The Ants)

إِنَّ هَـٰذَا ٱلْقُرْءَانَ يَقُصُّ عَلَىٰ بَنِىٓ إِسْرَٰٓءِيلَ أَكْثَرَ
ٱلَّذِى هُمْ فِيهِ يَخْتَلِفُونَ
٧٦

**Indeed, this Quran clarifies for the Children of
Israel most of what they differ over. (22:76)**

وَإِنَّهُۥ لَهُدًى وَرَحْمَةٌ لِّلْمُؤْمِنِينَ
٧٧

**And it is truly a guide and mercy for the believers.
(22:77)**

1

سورة ٱلأعراف
Surah Al-A'araaf (The Heights)

وَمِن قَوْمِ مُوسَىٰٓ أُمَّةٌ يَهْدُونَ بِٱلْحَقِّ وَبِهِۦ
يَعْدِلُونَ
١٥٩

There are some among the people of Moses who guide with the truth and establish justice accordingly. (7:159)

The book cover looks striking and deeply symbolic, showing a young Palestinian girl and a Jewish boy holding hands—an image that conveys unity, compassion, and shared humanity amidst conflict. The title, "The Pain I Feel For The Children Of Israel – 7th October & Beyond: An Islamic Perspective," combined with the serene background and harmonious expressions, makes a strong emotional and moral statement.

2

Table of Contents

Disclaimer

The views expressed in this book are solely the author's personal opinions and do not necessarily reflect those of the Qur'ani Murkuz Trust charity with which he is associated.

Also, any opinions expressed by any politicians or columnists mentioned in this book are solely their own views and do not necessarily reflect the convictions of the author.

Why did I write this book?

Out of the love I have for both the Children of Israel and the Palestinians, I decided to write this book to educate many people who are not aware of the persecution of the Children of Israel at the hands of many oppressors since the time of the ancient Egyptians until modern times.

I also wanted to share with many people who are not familiar with the suffering of the Palestinians, who have been forced out of their land since 1948 and the many massacres they have faced at the hands of their oppressors.

I wish that Hamas could have accepted the State of Israel and made peace with it, and Israel could have recognised Gaza as an independent demilitarised State and that they could have lived together side by side in peace. That was my sweet dream which became a nightmare after 7th October 2023.

The conflict in the Middle East has resulted in the loss of countless lives, and the horrific scenes witnessed since October 7, 2023, from Gaza and Israel have left millions of people around the world haunted by their memories. In light of these events, it is of utmost importance to gain a comprehensive understanding of what has transpired and what the future holds.

You have the right to disagree with me, but not the right to stifle debate and freedom of speech.

You may like this book or hate me but let us all pray: *"O God, The Most Merciful, The Most Compassionate, please help us all to establish an ever-lasting peace in the Middle East, in order that Jews and Arabs can live side by side in peace and harmony."*

Dedication

This book is dedicated to my ancestors, the remarkable ancient Egyptians who renounced their own religion and embraced the beliefs of Moses and Aaron.

Despite the immense sacrifices they endured, they stood in solidarity with the Children of Israel against the oppressive Pharaoh.

Who can forget the wife of Pharaoh, who carried baby Moses in her arms and pleaded with her husband, as recorded in Verse 28:9 in the Qur'an

(28:9): "Here is a delight for me and for you. Do not kill him. Perhaps he will be useful to us, or we may adopt him as a son."

When Moses became a Messenger of God, she immediately embraced the faith of Moses and expressed her devotion in Verse 66:11

(66:11): "My Lord, build for me a house near You in Paradise and save me from Pharaoh and his wickedness, and from the wrongdoers of the land."

Even the Egyptian magicians, who faced severe punishment from Pharaoh, chose to denounce him and believe in the Lord of Moses and Aaron.

After their defeat in the competition with Moses, they expressed their faith in Verse 20:73,

(20:73): "We believe in our Lord that He may forgive our sins and also forgive us the practice of magic that you (Pharaoh) compelled us to engage in. God is the Greatest, and He alone will endure."

I hold great admiration for the Egyptian man from the Pharaoh family who believed in Moses but concealed his faith to give himself an opportunity to preach to Pharaoh and his leaders, hoping to save them from God's wrath. He expressed his concern in Verse 40:29,

(40:29): "My people, today the kingdom is yours, and you are the supreme rulers of the land. But if God's punishment were to come upon you, who will come to our aid?"

If I had been born during the time of Moses, I would have undoubtedly believed in the One True God, the Lord of Moses and Aaron. I would have passionately spoken out against the injustices faced by the Children of Israel, just as I do today against the injustices inflicted on the innocent non-combatant Palestinians.

A message to the Secretary-General of the Muslim Council of Britain

Dear Secretary-General,

May Allah's Peace, Mercy and Blessings be upon you all.

I strongly urge every registered Muslim charity in the UK to read this book, particularly Chapter 19, which outlines the recommendations made by the Charity Commission, following the events in the Middle East on 7th October 2023.

For over 25 years, the trustees of our organisation, Qur'ani Murkuz Trust, have professionally managed the charity to ensure that it complies fully with the Charity Commission's rules and regulations. The inclusion of these recommendations in my book aims to help trustees of UK Muslim charities to become more familiar with their responsibilities to protect their charities.

Hostilities in Muslim countries, anywhere in the world, can sometimes influence UK Muslim charities, prompting emotional reactions that the Charity Commission may view as harmful. Such actions could trigger investigations, raise questions about the suitability of certain trustees, and even lead to the deregistration of the charity by the Commission.

Acknowledgements

At the very outset, I thank God the Almighty for guiding me and helping me to write this book.

I am deeply grateful to my very courageous, honest, and faithful Jewish brothers and sisters from the Board of Deputies of British Jews for their open letter dated 16th April 2025, to the Financial Times, which condemns the war in Gaza.

I would like to express my most sincere thanks to the late Abdullah Yusuf Ali for his great superlative work, "The Holy Qur'an: Text, Translation and Commentary". I have been studying his work since 1970. It is, by far, the best known, most studied and most respected English translation of The Qur'an. The authenticity of Yusuf Ali's extensive scholarly commentaries and explanatory notes and its distinguishing characteristics have been a great source of inspiration, not only to me, but also to many others. I have referred to many of his comments whilst writing this book. May God reward him abundantly, forgive all his sins and admit him to His Gardens of Bliss.

I would like to thank my fellow trustees at Qur'ani Murkuz Trust (QMT) for their guidance and support whilst writing this book.

I would like to thank Nadia Ali, Diana Al-Ghol, Tahsin Khan and Angela Haluk for their editorial work.

When it came to publishing the book, we explored many different avenues and concluded that the best way forward was to publish it on Amazon as an e-book and as a hard copy. This responsibility was taken by Mr Bilal Nawaz, whom I thank for his efforts.

I also thank my great granddaughter, Miss Noran Muhammad, for the amazing design of the cover of this book.

All proceeds from this book are donated to my Charity Qur'ani Murkuz Trust.

Introduction

My strife to propagate the peaceful message of Islam

I take immense pride in being a British Muslim of Egyptian heritage. The date Friday, 3rd July 1970, is etched in my memory, as it marks my arrival in the United Kingdom from Egypt at the age of 24. At the time, I was a young graduate in aeronautical engineering with three years of experience in the aircraft industry, eager to explore new opportunities and broaden my horizons.

My journey to the UK was initially to attend a three-month training course on a new computer system acquired by my Egyptian employer from International Computers Limited (ICL), the British counterpart to the American firm IBM. Upon completion of the course, my UK employer invited me to remain for an additional year to specialize in the development of computer applications for the construction industry using computer-aided design. This opportunity made me the first Egyptian to specialize in this emerging field of software.

During this formative period in the UK, I developed a deep appreciation for British values—democracy, the rule of law, civil liberties, freedom of speech and religion, equal opportunity, mutual respect, and tolerance. These values resonated profoundly with me, not only because they are fundamental to a cohesive and diverse society, but also because they align closely with the core principles of

Islam—though, regrettably, they are seldom upheld in many Muslim-majority countries. My admiration for these values was a significant factor in my decision to settle permanently in the UK, returning to Egypt only for brief visits to see family.

Growing up in Egypt, I had only encountered Egyptian Muslims of the Sunni tradition and Orthodox Egyptian Christians, who coexisted harmoniously. We attended the same schools and universities, lived in the same apartment blocks, and celebrated each other's religious occasions. Our shared humanity overshadowed any religious differences, and extremist ideologies were virtually non-existent. One common saying captured this spirit: "Religion belongs to God, and Egypt belongs to us all."

By the grace of God, I have been a practicing Muslim since childhood. My parents, both secularly and religiously educated, instilled in me a strong moral compass from a young age. They taught me to love and fear God in a balanced way, encouraging me to live a life of integrity rooted in divine values—a foundation that continues to guide me.

Before coming to the UK, I had never met a Jew, despite Egypt once having a significant Jewish population prior to 1956. My mother's dressmaker was Jewish, and she held her in high regard. I had also never encountered Hindus, Buddhists, Sikhs, atheists, or adherents of different Christian or Muslim denominations. Arriving in London was like stepping into a vibrant mosaic of cultures and beliefs—a "rainbow of humanity," as I often describe it. This diversity raised a profound question for me: how could I engage meaningfully with people of different faiths and cultures without compromising my own religious identity?

To answer this, I turned to the Qur'an and the teachings of Prophet Muhammad (peace be upon him), embarking on a personal journey of religious education and reflection. My pursuit of academic excellence—including a Master's in Computer Science from the University of London and a Doctorate from the London School of Economics in airport planning and design—did not deter me from my spiritual journey. One verse that continually inspired me is Qur'an 49:13:

(49:13): "O mankind! We created you from a single pair of a male and a female and made you into nations and tribes so that you may know one another—not despise one another. Verily, the most honoured among you in the sight of God is the most righteous. Indeed, God is All-Knowing, All-Aware."

This verse became the cornerstone of my interfaith engagement. I became actively involved in organisations such as Rotary International, the Multi-Faith Forum, and the Three Faiths Forum, where I had the honour of meeting people from all walks of life—believers and non-believers alike. As a mature student, I pursued formal studies in Chaplaincy and Muslim-Jewish relations at two UK universities. I also established a mosque in South Woodford, London, as part of my commitment to building bridges within and beyond the Muslim community.

Over the years, I have been invited to speak at several synagogues in London about Islam and Muslim-Jewish relations and have participated in numerous Holocaust memorial events as a guest speaker. I was humbled to be invited by the Israeli ambassador and the Chief Rabbi to share Iftar meals at their homes during the holy month of Ramadan.

Many of these experiences are chronicled in my book, Confused Muslims.Qom – Confessions of a London Imam, where I share the lessons, challenges, and insights I have gained in my ongoing journey to promote a peaceful, inclusive understanding of Islam in a multicultural society.

What do I believe in?

I am a believer who testifies to the following:

1.   I testify that there is no god but Allah Almighty the One and only God. He is the only One to whom worship is due. He is the Creator of the heavens and the earth, and everything hidden or seen. He has no equal. There is nothing like Him. He has no partner or associates in any form. He has no father, no mother, no wife and no children. He doesn't beget, nor He was begotten. He is near us. He is with us wherever we might be. He sees us and hears our supplications. He cares for us. We owe our existence to Him. He is Eternal, without beginning or end. He is Absolute, not limited by time or place or circumstances. He is the Most Gracious and the Most Merciful. He is the Lord of all the worlds. He is the Cherisher and Sustainer of all creatures. He is the King of the Day of Judgement. He is the One who accepts repentance, purges our sins and forgives us again and again. To Him belong the Most Beautiful Names and Attributes.

Allah tells us in verses 59:22-24, some of His Most Beautiful Names and Attributes.

(59:22): "He is Allah, there is no god but He, the Knower of the seen and the unseen. He is the Most Compassionate, the Most Merciful."

17

(59:23): "He is Allah, there is no god but He. He is the Sovereign, the Holy One, the Source of Peace, the Bestower of Security, the Guardian of Faith, the All-Mighty, the Overpowering Lord, the Sublime. Glorified be He from all that they ascribe as partner (to Him)!"

(59:24): "He is Allah, the Creator, the Originator, the Fashioner into shape, His are the Most Beautiful Names. All that is in the heavens and the earth glorifies Him, and He is the All-Mighty, the All-Wise."

2. I testify that I believe in all God's Angels as another creation by Him. They are not females or God's daughters.
3. I testify that I believe in all God's Divine Revelations He sent to His Messengers, including the Torah to Moses, the Psalms to David, the Bible to Jesus and the Qu'ran to Muhammad.
4. I testify that I believe in all God's Prophets and Messengers from Adam to Mohammed, including but not limited to, Noah, Abraham, Lut, Ishmail, Isaac, Jacob, Joseph, Moses, Aron, Ilyas, David, Solomon, Job, Jonah, Zakaria, John and Jesus. I testify that I do not make any distinction between any of them or associate any of them with God in any form.
   4.1. I testify that Moses is a Prophet and Messenger of God not His son.
   4.2. I testify that Jesus is a Prophet and Messenger of God not His son.
   4.3. I testify that Mohammed is the final and last Prophet and Messenger of God not His son.

5.   I testify that I believe in the Day of Judgement, Life after Death and the Unseen (the existence of that which is beyond the reach of perception).

6.   I testify that I believe and accept whatever God has willed and distended for me whether good or bad, without questioning Him. I submit my will to His Will and say, "I hear and obey".

Anyone who testifies to all the above is known, in Arabic, as a "Muslim". Islam means Peace and Absolute Submission to Allah the One and Only God. It is the religion of all the Prophets and Messengers of God from Adam to Muhammad, may God's Peace be upon all of them.

From a non-Muslim perspective this is slightly confusing as it is generally believed that Islam began with the Prophet Mohammed (pbuh). To explain this further, the word 'Islam' in the Holy Qur'an signifies that one religion that emerged in all divine revelations. God says in

(3:19): ""Indeed, the religion in the sight of God is Islam.......".

It refers to submitting one's will to God's Will, expressed through the phrase *"we hear and we obey."* Therefore, Adam was a Muslim because he surrendered his soul to the One True God. Similarly, Noah, Abraham, Ishmael, Isaac, Jacob, the Tribes, Moses, Jesus, and Muhammad, may God's peace be upon them all, were also Muslims.

However, the word 'Islam' was misused, leading to its gradual loss of its broad meaning and transformation into a reference to specific cultural identities.

The above "Testimony of Faith" is mentioned in many Verses in the Qur'an. I give below a few examples:

(3:33): "Indeed, God chose Adam and Noah and the family of Abraham and the family of Imran (the father of Mary) over all people."

(3:34): "Offspring, one of the other; and God hears and knows all things."
So, we must revere all these Prophets and Messengers because that was God's choice, as confirmed above.

In the next Verse 3:84, we as Muslims confess our faith:

(3:84): "Say, 'We have believed in God and in what was revealed to us and what was revealed to Abraham, Ishmael, Isaac, Jacob, and the Descendants, and in what was given to Moses and Jesus and to the prophets from their Lord. We make no distinction between any of them, and we are Muslims [submitting] to Him.'"

We are commanded in the following Verses 2:130-141, to follow the religion of Abraham:

(2:130): "And who would be averse to the religion of Abraham except one who makes a fool of himself. And We had chosen him in this world, and indeed he, in the Hereafter, will be among the righteous."

(2:131): "When his Lord said to him, 'Submit', he said 'I have submitted [in Islam] to the Lord of the worlds.'"

20

(2:132): "And Abraham instructed his sons [to do the same] and [so did] Jacob, [saying], 'O my sons, indeed God has chosen for you this religion, so do not die except while you are Muslims.'"

(2:133): "Or were you witnesses when death approached Jacob, when he said to his sons, 'What will you worship after me?' They said, 'We will worship your God and the God of your fathers, Abraham and Ishmael and Isaac - one God. And we are Muslims [in submission] to Him.'"

(2:134): "That was a nation which has passed on. It will have [the consequence of] what it earned, and you will have what you have earned. And you will not be asked about what they used to do."

(2:135): "They say, 'Be Jews or Christians [so] you will be guided.' Say, 'Rather, [we follow] the religion of Abraham, inclining toward truth, and he was not of the polytheists.'"

(2:136): "Say, [O believers], 'We have believed in God and what has been revealed to us and what has been revealed to Abraham and Ishmael and Isaac and Jacob and the Descendants and what was given to Moses and Jesus and what was given to the prophets from their Lord. We make no distinction between any of them, and we are Muslims [in submission] to Him.'"

(2:137): "So if they believe in the same as you believe in, then they have been [rightly] guided; but if they turn away, they are only in dissension, and God will be

sufficient for you against them. And He is the Hearing, the Knowing."

(2:138): "[And say, 'Ours is] the religion of God. And who is better than God in [ordaining] religion? And we are worshippers of Him.'"

(2:139): "Say, [O Muhammad], 'Do you argue with us about God while He is our Lord and your Lord? For us are our deeds, and for you are your deeds. And we are sincere [in deed and intention] to Him.'"

(2:140): "Or do you say that Abraham and Ishmael and Isaac and Jacob and the Descendants were Jews or Christians? Say, 'Are you more knowing or is God?' And who is more unjust than one who conceals a testimony he has from God? And God is not unaware of what you do."

(2:141): "That is a nation which has passed on. It will have [the consequence of] what it earned, and you will have what you have earned. And you will not be asked about what they used to do."

In Verses 3:65-67, God confirms that Abraham was neither a Jew nor a Christian, but he was a Muslim, who submitted his will to the Will of God.

(3:65): "O People of the Scripture, why do you argue about Abraham while the Torah and the Gospel were not revealed until after him? Then will you not reason?"

22

(3:66): "Here you are - those who have argued about that of which you have [some] knowledge, but why do you argue about that of which you have no knowledge? And God knows, while you know not."

(3:67): "Abraham was neither a Jew nor a Christian, but he was one inclining toward truth, a Muslim [submitting to Allah]. And he was not of the polytheists."

Are we ready for the Day of Judgement?

God commands us all to strive sincerely to obey His Moral Law as detailed in all His revealed Scriptures. Believing in the Day of Judgment, and life after death and that we will all be held accountable for everything we did in this life, should make us conscious of our conduct in this fleeting life.

For example, God tells us in Verses 18:49 and 21:47, that everything small or great will be recorded.

(18:49): "And the record [of deeds] will be placed [open], and you will see the criminals fearful of that within it, and they will say, 'Oh, woe to us! What is this book that leaves nothing small or great except that it has enumerated it? And they will find what they did present [before them]. And your Lord does injustice to no one."

(21:47): "And We place the scales of justice for the Day of Resurrection, so no soul will be treated unjustly at

*all. And if there is [even] the weight of a mustard seed,
We will bring it forth. And sufficient are We as
accountant."*

And whatever good or evil we do in this life, irrespective of
its size, we will reap its consequences on the Day of
Judgement, as stated in Verses 99:6-8:

*(99:6): "That Day, the people will depart separated
[into categories] to be shown [the result of] their
deeds."*

*(99:7): "So whoever does an atom's weight of good will
see it."*

*(99:8): "And whoever does an atom's weight of evil will
see it."*

Following God's Judgment on that Great Day, it will either
be eternal joy in Gardens of Bliss for those who feared
God in this life or eternal punishment in the Hellfire, for
those who forsook God.

God says in Verses 39:71-75:

*(39:71): "And those who disbelieved will be driven to
Hell in groups until, when they reach it, its gates are
opened and its keepers will say, 'Did there not come to
you messengers from yourselves, reciting to you the
verses of your Lord and warning you of the meeting of
this Day of yours?' They will say, 'Yes', but the word of
punishment has come into effect upon the
disbelievers."*

(39:72): "[To them] it will be said, 'Enter the gates of Hell to abide eternally therein, and wretched is the residence of the arrogant.'"

(39:73): "But those who feared their Lord will be driven to Paradise in groups until, when they reach it while its gates have been opened and its keepers say, 'Peace be upon you; you have become pure; so enter it to abide eternally therein,' [they will enter]."

(39:74): "And they will say, 'Praise to God, who has fulfilled for us His promise and made us inherit the earth [so] we may settle in Paradise wherever we will. And excellent is the reward of [righteous] workers.'"

(39:75): "And you will see the angels surrounding the Throne, exalting [God] with praise of their Lord. And it will be judged between them in truth, and it will be said, '[All] praise to God, Lord of the worlds.'"

God describes in Verses 4:56, the painful doom and the eternal suffering of those who forsook Him in this life, and in Verse 4:57, He gives glad tidings to the righteous.

(4:56): "Indeed, those who disbelieve in Our verses - We will drive them into a Fire. Every time their skins are roasted through We will replace them with other skins so they may taste the punishment. Indeed, Allah is ever Exalted in Might and Wise."

(4:57): "But those who believe and do righteous deeds - We will admit them to gardens beneath which rivers flow, wherein they abide forever. For them therein are

purified spouses, and We will admit them to deepening shade."

I believe it is important to explain to the reader the concept of the Day of Judgment and life after death in Judaism and Christianity.

Judaism and Christianity share a concept of an afterlife, often referred to as "the world to come" or "olam ha-ba." Jewish texts, particularly the Talmud, discuss various afterlife destinations, such as Gan Eden (paradise) and Gehinnom (a place of punishment).

The belief in resurrection, where the dead will rise again, is also a core Jewish belief, especially in relation to the coming of the Messiah.

While the concept of a specific Day of Judgment is not as prominent in Judaism as in some other religions, Jewish tradition emphasises that our actions in this life will have consequences. Jewish denominations and individuals hold diverse views on the nature of the afterlife and the process of judgment.

However, Judaism places significant emphasis on living a righteous and meaningful life in this world, viewing it as a crucial preparation for whatever awaits us in the afterlife.

In essence, while the Torah explicitly does not describe a specific "Day of Judgment," the Jewish faith acknowledges the existence of a life beyond death, with some form of reward or punishment for our actions in this world.

The Christian scriptures, particularly the New Testament, explicitly mention both life after death and a Day of Judgment. Hebrews 9:27 states, "it is appointed unto men once to die, after which cometh the judgment," implying a time of reckoning after death. Revelation 20:12-15 describes a final judgment where the dead, both believers and unbelievers, will be judged according to their deeds.

In this book, religion, politics, history, the past, and the present are all intricately connected.

In my analysis, I will refer to the Verses of the Qur'an which mention the persecution of the Children of Israel in ancient Egypt by Pharaoh and his Chiefs and their persecution, later in modern history, at the hands of other oppressors. I will also refer to the prophecy of what will happen, until the Day of Judgment, to those among the Children of Israel who would blaspheme and become secular and violate the teachings of the Torah and reject faith.

In addition to the above, I shall include:
- The statement I read out on Friday 13th October 2024, condemning the killing of innocent Israeli civilians by Hamas on 7th October 2023, and condemning the Israeli attacks on Gaza killing innocent non-combatant men, women and children.
- The transcript of my Friday sermon on 13th October 2023, covering the topic "How does God deal with the oppressors?"
- The shocking response to my sermon by the National Secular Society (NSS).

- The communication between the Political Editor of the Sunday Telegraph and the South Woodford Islamic Centre concerning the above.
- The highlights of the communication we had with the Charity Commission (CC).
- The statements made by many European and Arab politicians who stated that there will be no peace in the region and Israel will never feel safe if it does not end the occupation, stop the building of illegal settlements and accept the two-state solution.

In my analysis, I will refer to the footnotes written by the great Muslim scholar Abdullah Yusuf Ali (1872-1953) in his inspiring publication: "The Holy Qur'an: Text, Translation and Commentary". A verse will be indicated by giving the chapter number followed by the verse number. Whilst a footnote will be shown as FN followed by the number.

An example of this is as follows:

(7:128): "And Moses said to his people, 'Seek help through God and be patient. Indeed, the earth belongs to God. He causes to inherit it whom He wills of His servants. And the [best] outcome is for the righteous' (1085)."

"Notice the contrast between the arrogant tone of Pharaoh and the humility and faith taught by Moses. In the end the arrogance was humbled, and humility and faith were protected and advanced." (FN1085)

In the text, I will replace the Arabic word "Allah", by the English word "God".

Who was Israel?

Israel is another name of Prophet Jacob as stated by God in Verse 3:93 in the Qur'an and in many verses when God is addressing his children by saying: "O Children of Israel". Jacob was the son of Isaac, who was the son of Abraham. Isaac was the brother of Ismael. Jacob had 12 sons, they are referred to in the Qur'an in Verses 2:136 and 3:84 as Al-Asbaat, "the Tribes" or "the Descendants". They were all Prophets of God. They are also referred to by God in the Quran as "Banu Israel", "the Sons of Israel". However, they are referred to in English translations as "the Children of Israel".

Believers amongst the Muslims must accept what is stated in the following verses and submit their will fully to God's Will, as previously mentioned.

(2:136): "Say, [O believers], 'We have believed in God and what has been revealed to us and what has been revealed to Abraham and Ishmael and Isaac and Jacob and the Descendants and what was given to Moses and Jesus and what was given to the prophets from their Lord. We make no distinction between any of them, and we are Muslims [in submission] to Him.'"

(3:84): "Say, 'We have believed in God and in what was revealed to us and what was revealed to Abraham, Ishmael, Isaac, Jacob, and the Descendants, and in what was given to Moses and Jesus and to the prophets from their Lord. We make no distinction between any of them, and we are Muslims [submitting] to Him.'"

(4:163): "Indeed, We have revealed to you, [O Muhammad], as We revealed to Noah and the prophets after him. And we revealed to Abraham, Ishmael, Isaac, Jacob, the Descendants, Jesus, Job, Jonah, Aaron, and Solomon, and to David We gave the book [of Psalms]."

(4:164): "And [We sent] messengers about whom We have related [their stories] to you [Muhammad] before and messengers about whom We have not related to you. And God spoke to Moses with [direct] speech."

(4:165): "[We sent] messengers as bringers of good tidings and warners so that mankind will have no argument against God after the messengers. And ever is God Exalted in Might and Wise."

(4:166): "But God bears witness to that which He has revealed to you [Muhammad]. He has sent it down with His knowledge, and the angels bear witness [as well]. And sufficient is Allah as Witness."

We are told in Verse 2:133, that when Jacob was on his deathbed in Ancient Egypt, and while he was surrounded by his 12 sons, he enjoined his legacy on them:

(2:133): "Or were you witnesses when death approached Jacob, when he said to his sons, 'What will you worship after me?' They said, 'We will worship your God and the God of your fathers, Abraham and Ishmael and Isaac - one God. And we are Muslims [in submission] to Him.'"

So, Jacob felt so relieved as he had fully discharged his responsibility as a father to ensure that his 12 sons, who were already Prophets of God, would continue to worship the One True God.

Where did Prophet Abraham come from?

Abraham was an emigrant who fled from the persecution in his own country and moved to Hebron, in the Holy Land, and settled there with his wife Sara.

He was born in Ur of the Chaldees, a place on the lower reaches of the Euphrates, not a hundred miles from the Persian Gulf, known as the cradle, or one of the cradles, of human civilisation. Astronomy was studied here in very ancient times, and the worship of the sun, moon, and stars were the prevailing form of religion. Abraham revolted against this quite early in life, and his argument is referred to in 6:74-82, in the Qur'an.. They also had idols in their temples, probably idols representing heavenly bodies and celestial winged creatures. He was still a youth (21:60) when he broke the idols.

This was stage No. 2. After this he was marked down as a rebel and persecuted. Perhaps some years passed before the incident of his being thrown into the Fire (21:68-69) took place, or the incident may be only allegorical. Traditionally the Fire incident is referred to a king called Nimrud, about whom see FN1565 to Verse 11:69. If Nimrud 's capital was in Assyria, near Nineveh (site near modern Mosul, in Iraq), we may suppose either that the king's rule extended over the whole of Mesopotamia, or that Abraham wandered north through Babylonia to Assyria.Various stratagems were devised to get rid of him (21:70), but he was saved by the mercy of God. The final break came when he was probably a man of mature age and could speak to his father with some authority. This incident is referred to in 19:41-48. He now left his ancestral lands, and avoiding the Syrian desert, came to the fertile lands of Aram or Syria, and south to Canaan, when the incident of 11:69-76 and the adventures of his nephew Lut took place. It is some years after this that we may suppose he built the Ka'bah (the House of God in Makkah), with the help of his eldest son Isma'i1 (2:124-129), and his prayer in 14:35-41 may be referred to the same time. His visit to Egypt (Gen.12:10) is not referred to in the Qur'an.

Following his visit to Egypt, he took Hajar as a wife and he had Isma'il as his first son at the age of 86 according to the Bible. Abraham took his baby son Isma'il and his mother Hajer and travelled to Makkah and left them there. This is in accordance with Islamic tradition.When Abraham was 100 years old, his wife Sara gave birth to Issac, as mentioned in the Bible. So, neither Abraham, nor his wife Sara, nor their son Isaac and their grandson Jacob were natives of the Holy Land. They were all emigrants.

Chapter One - My tears at Yad Vashem Museum

In collaboration with my esteemed brother Rabbi D.H., we have organised numerous trips to the Holy Land, inviting a diverse group of Muslims, Jews, and Christians to explore Israel and Palestine.

When I arrived at Ben Gurion Airport in Tel Aviv, Israel, for the first time in my life, I was filled with a mixture of anxiety and excitement. This was a country we had been at war with for many years, and now I was visiting with great joy. The credit for this opportunity for peace in the Middle East goes to the late President Sadat of Egypt.

At passport control, a very young officer asked me, while holding my passport in her hand, "What is your name?" I replied, "Muhammad." She then asked, "And your father's name?" I said, "Muhammad." She continued, "And your grandfather's name?" I said, "Muhammad Fahim." Finally, she asked me about my place of birth. I said, "Monofia". She asked: "Where is Monofia?" I said "Egypt". Unfortunately, the information on a British passport is so limited.

She said: "I can't handle your passport. Go to that room there."

When I entered the room, it was packed with people. I was so exhausted because our flight had been overnight, and I had barely slept. I waited and waited, and after a long time, a man came in holding a passport in his hand. He said: "Muhammad Muhammad Muhammad Fahim."

I raised my hand and said, "Yes." He then asked from the far end of the room, "Where is Monofia?" Honestly, I couldn't control myself because the details of our passports had already been sent to them before our flight from London. So, I screamed at him, "Monofia is where the late President Sadat was born, and the current President Mubarak was born. I am the future President of Egypt!" The poor man said "We know Egypt, but not Monofia," and then he gave me my passport and let me go.

When I arrived at the baggage hall and met with the rest of the group, I was struck by two large photographs adorning the wall. They depicted the late President Sadat and other Egyptian and Israeli politicians. It was a surprising sight, as if the current Israeli government was acknowledging the bravery of the Arab and Muslim world's most courageous president.

Inspired by this unexpected display, I decided to delve into the historic and courageous speech delivered by late President Sadat on November 20th, 1977, at the Israeli Knesset.

This speech played a pivotal role in paving the way for a comprehensive peace agreement between Israel and Egypt. Following President Sadat's impassioned words, Israeli Prime Minister Begin took the stage to represent Israel and reaffirmed its unwavering desire and willingness to forge a lasting peace with Egypt.

Below is a concise summary of the last part of the speech by late Egyptian President Sadat.

"An Edifice of Peace

Why don't we stand together with the courage of men and the boldness of heroes who dedicated themselves to a sublime aim? Why don't we stand together with the same courage and daring to erect a huge edifice of peace?

An edifice that builds and does not destroy. An edifice that serves as a beacon for generations to come with the human message for construction, development, and the dignity of man.

Why should we bequeath to the coming generations the plight of bloodshed, yes, orphans, widowhood, family disintegration, and the wailing of victims?

Why don't we believe in the wisdom of God conveyed to us by the wisdom of the proverbs of Solomon? [Mr. Sadat went on to quote extensively from the proverbs.]

Ladies and gentlemen, to tell you the truth, peace cannot be worth its name unless it is based on justice and not on the occupation of the land of others. It would not be right for you to demand for yourselves what you deny to others. With all frankness and in the spirit that has prompted me to come to you today, I tell you: you have to give up once and for all the dreams of conquest and give up the belief that force is the best method for dealing with the Arabs.

You should clearly understand the lesson of confrontation between you and us. Expansion does not pay. To speak frankly, our land does not yield itself to bargaining; it is not even open to argument. To us, the nation's soil is equal to the holy valley where God Almighty spoke to Moses. Peace be upon him. We cannot accept any attempt to take away or accept to seek one inch of it, nor can we accept the principle of debating or bargaining over it.

I sincerely tell you also that before us today lies the appropriate chance for peace. If we are really serious in our endeavour for peace, it is a chance that may never come again. It is a chance that if lost or wasted, the resulting slaughter would bear the curse of humanity and of history.

What is peace for Israel? It means that Israel lives in the region with her Arab neighbours in security and safety. Is this logical? I say yes. It means that Israel lives within its borders, secure against any aggression. Is that logical? And I say yes. It means that Israel obtains all kinds of guarantees that will ensure these two factors. To this demand, I say yes.

Beyond that, we declare that we accept all the international guarantees you envisage and accept. We declare that we accept all the guarantees you want from the two superpowers or from either of them or from the Big Five or from some of them.

Once again, I declare clearly and unequivocally that we agree to any guarantees you accept because in return, we shall receive the same guarantees.

In short, then, when we ask what is peace for Israel, the answer would be that Israel lives within her borders,

*among her Arab neighbours in safety and security, within
the framework of all the guarantees she accepts and which
are offered to her.*

*But, how can this be achieved? How can we reach this
conclusion which would lead us to permanent peace based
on justice? There are facts that should be faced with
courage and clarity. There are Arab territories which Israel
has occupied and still occupies by force. We insist on
complete withdrawal from these territories, including Arab
Jerusalem.*

*I have come to Jerusalem, the city of peace, which will
always remain as a living embodiment of coexistence
among believers of the three religions. It is inadmissible
that anyone should conceive the special status of the city
of Jerusalem within the framework of annexation or
expansionism. It should be a free and open city for all
believers.*

*Above all, this city should not be severed from those who
have made it their abode for centuries. Instead of reviving
the precedent of the Crusades, we should revive the spirit
of Omar ibn El Khtab and Saladin, namely the spirit of
tolerance and respect for right.*

*The holy shrines of Islam and Christianity are not only
places of worship but a living testimony of our interpreted
presence here. Politically, spiritually, and intellectually,
here let us make no mistake about the importance and
reverence we Christians and Moslems attach to
Jerusalem.*

Let me tell you without the slightest hesitation that I have not come to you under this roof to make a request that your troops evacuate the occupied territories. Complete withdrawal from the Arab territories occupied after 1967 is a logical and undisputed fact. Nobody should plead for that. Any talk about permanent peace based on justice and any move to ensure our coexistence in peace and security in this part of the world would become meaningless while you occupy Arab territories by force of arms.

For there is no peace that could be built on the occupation of the land of others; otherwise, it would not be a serious peace. Yet this is a foregone conclusion which is not open to the passion of debate if intentions are sincere or if endeavours to establish a just and durable peace for our and for generations to come are genuine.

As for the Palestine cause — nobody could deny that it is the crux of the entire problem. Nobody in the world could accept today's slogans propagated here in Israel, ignoring the existence of a Palestinian people and questioning even their whereabouts. Because the Palestine people and their legitimate rights are no longer denied today by anybody: that is, nobody who has the ability of judgment can deny or ignore it.

It is an acknowledged fact, perceived by the world community, both in the East and in the West, with support and recognition in international documents and official statements. It is of no use to anybody to turn a deaf ear to its resounding voice, which is being heard day and night, or to overlook its historical reality.

Even the United States of America, your first ally, which is absolutely committed to safeguarding Israel's security and existence and which offered and still offers Israel every moral, material, and military support — I say, even the United States has opted to face up to reality and admit that the Palestinian people are entitled to legitimate rights and that the Palestine problem is the cause and essence of the conflict and that so long as it continues to be unresolved, the conflict will continue to aggravate, reaching new dimensions.

In all sincerity, I tell you that there can be no peace without the Palestinians. It is a grave error of unpredictable consequences to overlook or brush aside this cause.

I shall not indulge in past events such as the Balfour Declaration 60 years ago. You are well acquainted with the relevant text. If you have found the moral and legal justification to set up a national home on a land that did not all belong to you, it is incumbent upon you to show understanding of the insistence of the people of Palestine for establishment once again of a state on their land. When some extremist asks the Palestinians to give up this sublime objective, this in fact means asking them to renounce their identity and every hope for the future.

I hail the Israeli voices that called for the recognition of the Palestinian people's right to achieve and safeguard peace.

Here I tell you, ladies and gentlemen, that it is no use to refrain from recognising the Palestinian people and their right to statehood as their right of return. We, the Arabs, have faced this experience before, with you. And with the reality of the Israeli existence, the struggle which took us from war to war, from victims to more victims, until you and we have today reached the edge of a horrible abyss and a terrifying disaster unless, together, we seize this opportunity today of a durable peace based on justice."

At Yad Vashem Museum (A Hand and a Name)

During my visit to Israel, I made a solemn pilgrimage to the Holocaust Memorial Museum, "Yad Vashem," which stands as a poignant reminder of the atrocities committed against innocent Jews during the Holocaust.

The sheer depth of my sorrow and grief was overwhelming as I confronted the haunting images and videos that depicted the persecution of Jews by their Nazi adversaries. Tears streamed down my face as I witnessed the inhumanity inflicted upon innocent women and children, who were forcibly removed from their homes and sent to concentration camps. The question of why such cruelty was perpetrated against fellow human beings left me deeply troubled.

This experience brought to mind the Spanish Inquisition (1478–1834), a period of religious persecution that targeted Jews and Muslims for their faith. The echoes of that dark chapter serve as a grim reminder of the dangers of intolerance and discrimination.

Regrettably, Muslim minorities in non-Muslim countries continue to face discrimination, persecution, and even death for their beliefs.

One British Jewish friend once expressed a profound sentiment, stating, "Muslims and Jews must unite. If one group falls, the other will follow."

This sentiment is echoed in the Qur'an, where God emphasises the interconnectedness of human life and the consequences of actions. Verse 5:32 states,

(5:32): "Because of this (murder), We ordained for the Children of Israel that if anyone slew a person—unless it be (in punishment) for murder or for spreading mischief in the land— it would be as if he slew all mankind; and if anyone saved a life it would be as if he had given life to all mankind. Then although came to them Our Messengers with clear Signs, yet even after that many of them continued to commit excesses in the land."

The same teachings are found in the Jewish Scripture, the Talmud. I firmly believe that we are all brothers and sisters in humanity, regardless of our ethnicity, religion, or gender, as stated by God in Verse 49:13, which I have previously mentioned and will reiterate here

(49:13): "O mankind! We created you all from a single pair of a male and a female, and made you into nations and tribes, so that you may get to know each other (not that you may despise each other). Verily the most honoured of you in the sight of God is (he who is) the most righteous of you. And God has full knowledge and is well acquainted (with all things)."

God further states in Verses 109:1-6

(109:1-6): "Say: 'O unbelievers! I do not worship what you worship. Nor do you worship what I worship. Nor will I (ever) worship what you worship. Nor will you worship what I worship. To you your religion and to me, my religion.'"

These verses define the appropriate attitude towards those who reject faith. While we cannot compromise on matters of truth, there is no need to persecute or abuse anyone for their religious beliefs. Therefore, irrespective of our religions and none, we must continue to accept each other, tolerate each other, and live together in peace and harmony, as we are all descendants of Adam and Eve.

During their 1919 revolution against British occupation, Egyptians used to proclaim: "Religion belongs to God, and Egypt belongs to everyone" to unite Muslims, Christians, and Jews against the occupiers.

Chapter Two - Joseph, the Saviour of Egypt, and the arrival of Israel in Egypt

The story of Prophet Jacob (Israel) and his twelve sons, as mentioned in Chapter 12 of the Holy Qur'an, inspired me to publish my first book. The title of the book is "A Father's Journey and a Son's Dream: The Story of Joseph, the Son of Jacob".

The story gives us the history of how the Children of Israel moved from the desert of Canaan to settle in the prosperous ancient Egypt, which unfortunately, later became a source of pain and misery to them.

The story is about a large family which was torn into pieces by jealousy and hatred. The father Jacob and his son Joseph managed to put a very confusing and complicated jigsaw together to restore the family unit. I admire the way in which both Jacob and his son Joseph dealt with the other ten jealous Children of Israel. The first chapter of my book narrates the spiritual journeys which Jacob had to travel, in order to fulfil the dream of his son Joseph and to save the rest of the Children of Israel from God's wrath.

Both Joseph and Jacob had suffered for a long time from the evil planning and plotting practiced by these ten men. However, the father and his son each had a different plan to follow to save the souls of the Children of Israel.

From his position as a slave, Joseph became the Minister in charge of the Egyptian economy. He worked relentlessly hard to save Egypt from a seven-year famine. He also supported his family back in Canaan without them knowing who he was.

Eventually, the evil brothers repented and became good, and the entire family set off for Egypt to be reunited with Joseph.

I give below the highlights of this captivating story. But please, no one should blame Joseph for not getting united with his ailing father immediately after being freed from prison and becoming the minister in charge of the Egyptian economy. Joseph was diligently following God's divine guidance to save the Children of Israel from God's punishment.

Act I: Divine Visions

One beautiful, fresh morning, Joseph woke to hear the birds singing their rich songs of praise to God. Among the birds greeting the newborn day were two snow-white rock doves, their shining bodies appearing translucent against the bright sun. Joseph lay watching them and thinking about a strange and beautiful vision he had experienced during the night.As soon as he woke up, he knew that the dream was important...

In his dream, Joseph was dressed in fine clothes. He had watched in amazement as the sun, the moon, and eleven stars bowed down before him. It was all very strange. When he awoke, he ran to tell his father Jacob, who gazed tenderly at him and said, 'What a glorious dream, my beloved son. May God always bless you.'

Jacob loved his two youngest boys, Joseph and Benjamin, very much and gave them more attention than he did to the others, especially when the death of Rachel left them without a mother to look after them. The other ten brothers, knowing their father's great love for Joseph and Benjamin, had become very jealous.

Jacob was a wise, religious man who could see that Joseph, even as a child, was full of the Spirit of God.He foresaw that among all his sons, it was Joseph who would be chosen by God for a very special destiny.

The ten half-brothers had been led astray by Satan, the evil force that had put unkind and selfish thoughts into their minds. Their jealousy might make them plot against Joseph and harm him. So, when Joseph told Jacob about the dream, his father became afraid for him and begged his son not to mention the dream to his brothers.

Jacob warned Joseph about his danger and said to him, 'My dear little son, don't relate your vision to your brothers, lest they plot evil against you. Satan is the sworn enemy of man. You may not understand the meaning of your vision now, but God will choose you and teach you to interpret visions. He is All-Wise and All-Knowing. Have faith in Him, as your forefathers Isaac and Abraham did.'

Act II: The Well

The ten older brothers envied and hated Joseph and Benjamin. Jacob had the wisdom to see that his two young and innocent sons needed protection and that Joseph, in particular, had spiritual greatness within him. But to his ten other sons, Jacob's wisdom was only folly or madness because it opposed their own sense of self-love, as the truth often does. Thus, they relied on the brute strength of numbers—the ten hefty brethren against Jacob, Joseph, and Benjamin— in order to carry out their evil plot.

The ten brothers were watching from a distance with jealousy and hatred in their eyes when they saw Joseph and Benjamin sitting on their father's knee.

'We are just as good as those two; our father is an old fool!' whispered one of the brothers. 'We are always being told, 'Why can't you be good like Joseph!' He is always talking about Joseph. He has no consideration at all for our hard work.'

'Something will have to be done,' another brother said. 'We will have to get rid of Joseph. Kill him or cast him out to some unknown land. There will be plenty of time to turn over a new leaf later. Once Joseph is out of the way, we can make a good impression on our father and he will love and favour us as much as he loves and favours Joseph now.'

'Don't kill Joseph, said the older brother, who was perhaps a little kinder than the others, or perhaps he simply did not want to be accused of murder. 'Let us leave him at the

46

bottom of a well north of here. Then we will not be guilty of having his blood on our hands and maybe some travellers passing by will find him and take him to a far country. Whatever happens, at least we will be rid of him without actually killing him.'

The others agreed. 'At least this way we will not be responsible for his death. And later we can pretend to be good like him, or to repent of our crime after we have had all its benefits.' Sadly, Satan made their sinful acts seem alluring to them.

They went to see their father.

'Father, will you allow Joseph to come with us tomorrow? He can enjoy himself and play, and we shall take every care of him.'
They saw Jacob's reluctance. He did not know what was in their minds, but he had strong suspicions.

'I shall miss him if you take him with you, and I shall worry about him. Suppose a wolf comes and drags him away while you are busy and not looking after him?' Jacob said.

'Don't you trust us?' replied the eldest. 'There are ten of us. Surely the wolf would have to get past us before it could get near Joseph.'

Then Joseph pleaded with his father, 'Please, I should like to go.'

Although he loved his father dearly, he was also anxious to prove that he too could go on a journey like his brothers.

Jacob hesitated and then agreed, persuaded by the brothers' arguments and by Joseph's plea.

It was hot the next day when the party set off with Joseph running ahead. After some hours they reached the well and stopped to rest. After they had eaten, they played games and ran races. Joseph was beginning to tire and the oldest brother said, 'Come and sit by me and have a rest.' While Joseph slept the brothers schemed and, in low voices, discussed what to do. They devised a cunning plan. The eldest son shook Joseph awake.

Joseph, wake up! I've lost the ring Father gave me. It dropped into the well. If we lowered you in the bucket, could you try and find it for us?

Joseph was by far the lightest and smallest and the obvious one to choose for this difficult task, so without any suspicion of their real motives, he gladly did what his brothers asked. Yet when the bucket reached the bottom, the brothers cut the rope. At first, Joseph thought that the rope had broken and somehow his brothers would rescue him, even as their voices faded away. There was little light and the walls were wet and cold. For a while Joseph believed his brothers would return but, as the hours passed, he realised that they had left him to die. The only comfort left to him was his faith in the love and mercy of God. His spirit remained strong and his courage did not fail him. Indeed it was now, when the situation seemed hopeless, that God comforted him by putting into his heart the idea that, someday, his brothers would need him; that one day Joseph would be in a position to help them and that he would do so gladly, making them ashamed of the way they were treating him now.

The brothers returned home in the early part of the night, ready with a tale they had invented to explain to their father why Joseph had not come back with them. It was dark and Jacob dimly saw the faces of his ten sons as he looked anxiously for Joseph. They pretended to weep as they spoke.

'Father, we were having a race and we left Joseph to look after our things. When we returned, a wolf had dragged him away and devoured him. We know you don't believe us, even though we are telling the truth.'

Jacob staggered, as if from a blow. He shook his head in disbelief.

'O my beloved son, my dear one!'

As proof, the eldest brother held up the coat Joseph had worn. The coat of beautiful colours that Jacob had given him, the coat they had stained red with an animal's blood.

'It is the truth', they said.

Jacob held the coat to him and slowly sank to his knees. He looked up at them in despair.

'No, I cannot believe you. You have made up this tale. Your souls have tempted you to do something evil. Ah! What is there left for me now that my beloved son has gone?'

But even in his despair, Jacob's faith was strong. 'I ask God for patience. Only God can help me to bear the loss you speak of.'

In fact, Jacob had two options: either to behave in a godly way or to condemn, disown, and throw out his children, as many parents of today may have done. In choosing the former option, Jacob embarked on a long-term rehabilitation plan to bring his children back to God's Straight Path. Jacob knew that the best way to save his children from God's anger was to persevere patiently, have faith in God's soothing mercy, and to always maintain communication with his children.

The following day, when the sun was in the middle of the sky, a caravan of travellers reached the well where Joseph was; naturally, their first task was to draw water. Deep in the well, Joseph heard them talking as a bucket came down towards him.

Although he was exhausted and weak from hunger, he managed to catch hold of the bucket. He clung tight to it and felt himself slowly being raised to the surface. Imagine the merchants' surprise when this heavy bucket produced not water but a young and handsome boy.

'This is amazing! What good fortune,' they exclaimed.

'Here is a fine boy who does not belong to anyone and whom we can sell for a large sum of money in the Slave market in Egypt. What a treasure!'

Suddenly, there was a noise behind him. Two of Joseph's brothers had returned to the spot and had been watching to see what would happen to him.

'This boy belongs to us,' said one. 'He is a runaway slave. We were looking for him.'

What an evil statement made by this brother! Poor Joseph, how did he feel? It was his faith that prevented him from responding. Joseph now realised that home was a dangerous place; it was safer to be a slave than it was to be alone with his brothers.

Despite the anguish this must have caused him, Joseph knew that all that God wills is for the best.

The travellers thought the older brother's story was unlikely, but asked anyway, 'What do you intend to do with him?'

The brothers hesitated and looked at one another. 'He's more trouble than he's worth; it's time we got rid of him', they said.

They settled on a miserable price and so Joseph was sold into slavery for a handful of silver coins.

Now we can see how everyone in this story reacted differently according to their limited view of the situation. Joseph, in spite of his faith, must have felt hurt at his brothers' betrayal. Jacob, though patient, was sunk in grief at the loss of the son he loved so much. The brothers, delighted with the success of their plan, had managed to get rid of Joseph. Finally, the merchants were congratulating themselves on acquiring a handsome youth at such a bargain. All of them only saw part of the picture. God, who knows everything, knew all their feelings, motives, and deeds, was working out His own plan. None of us know where our destiny is leading us; we cannot see how, in God's plan, evil will eventually be defeated and good will overcome everything. None of us had any choice before coming to this life. We do not know when or how or where we are going to die. We cannot even push death away or ask for respite when it comes to us. So, the wise person is the one who believes in the One True God, does not associate any partners with Him in any form, strives patiently, and performs good deeds in this life to achieve salvation in the hereafter. That was the plan of Jacob and Joseph, both of whom put their full trust in God to defeat Satan the Evil One and save the Children of Israel who were destined to carry the torch of God into the Holy Land.

Act III: The Palace

So, the caravan, taking Joseph as a slave, travelled on towards Egypt. The merchants were not mistaken; there were indeed many people ready to bid for this handsome, intelligent youth. There was great competition to buy him, but all were outbid by an honourable lord, a great Egyptian court dignitary.

The lord was elderly and childless. When he saw Joseph, the idea came to him that he could buy Joseph as a slave and then perhaps later adopt him as his son. By having a son like Joseph, he would gain dignity and esteem at the court. Therefore, the lord bought Joseph from the merchants and took him back to his palace, where he presented him to his wife Zulaikha.

'Make his stay among us good and honourable,' he told her, 'maybe he will bring us good fortune.
Perhaps we shall adopt him as a son.'

This is the miracle of God's plan. From being sold into slavery at the well, Joseph was now established in a noble home in Egypt. God has full power over all things. However, most people do not know this.

Zulaikha was very young and loved her husband as a daughter loves a father. As she looked at Joseph, she was reminded of a man she had seen in a dream long ago, a dream she had kept secret and cherished in her heart. In her dream, she had been promised that this was the man she would marry.

Some years passed and Joseph grew from a youth to a young man. Although he grew up in the most luxurious surroundings at the Egyptian court, he also witnessed the corruption, the struggle for power, and the immorality of life in the palace.

Despite this, he kept his qualities of dignity and modesty and was honest and truthful in all that he did. God bestowed on him sound judgement and knowledge, as God will always reward those who do good deeds.

In this way, God established Joseph in Egypt, so that He might teach him to see the reality behind dreams and events. Through Joseph, the people of Egypt and the whole world would learn of the goodness and the wisdom of God.

But Zulaikha, remembering the young man of her dream and witnessing how Joseph grew in goodness and nobility, came to love him more and more. Gradually her love for him overwhelmed her. She found excuses for herself in her mind; I am not really the lord's wife. He is my husband in name only. He is more like a father to me. I am sure that Joseph loves me. I must have him. Surely these were immoral thoughts!

One evening, she ordered Joseph to come to her room. Her heart thudding, her body trembling, she shut the door behind him and locked it in haste. Turning to face him, she said, You know that I love you. Come my dear one. Take me. I'm all yours.'

Joseph stepped back startled. 'God forbid! Your husband is my master and has been so good to me, treating me like a son. I must be faithful to him and so must you. What you are asking me to do is wrong, and no good will ever come of it'

His plea had no effect on her; she was completely overwhelmed by her passion for him. Indeed, he too, as a human being with natural human emotions, would have given in to her, but he knew that it was wrong. She thought that no one could see behind closed doors, but he knew that God sees everything and his faith guided him. But there was no point in arguing with her.
'I must go', he said, and made quickly for the door.

Zulaikha ran after him, tearing his shirt as she tried to pull him back.

Joseph managed to open the door and came suddenly to a halt. Outside the door were his master, the lora, and a young boy who was Zulaikha's cousin.

There was a shocked silence. Then Zulaikha cried, 'He tried to assault me. You must put him in prison or flog him. He must be punished severely for trying to seduce your wife.'

'It was she who tried to seduce me.' Joseph spoke with quiet dignity and truth, without anger or bitterness.

Then the young boy, who had been looking carefully at all that was happening, said with the clear-sightedness and frankness of a child, 'If his shirt is torn at the front, then her tale is true and he is a liar, but if his shirt is torn from the back, then he must be telling the truth and she is a liar.' Amazing judgement! That this child could think so logically in such a tense situation!

When the lord saw that the shirt was indeed torn from the back, he knew Joseph had spoken the truth.

Now he had to decide what to do. As a high-ranking officer of state, he was in a very difficult position as such a scandal would likely undermine his high status in society. He was an old man, who had improved his own dignity and rank by marrying this noble and beautiful princess. She was young and impetuous, but he was sure that Joseph was innocent.

'I know you women and your tricks. Your evil planning is great indeed. Joseph, please do not tell anyone about this incident. My wife, ask for forgiveness for your sin for truly you have been at fault.'

Zulaikha was bitter and humiliated. How can my husband possibly understand my feelings for Joseph? She said to herself.
Joseph was true to his promise not to tell anyone about the incident, but Zulaikha was unable to keep silent. Rumours of the scene at the palace quickly began to spread through the city and soon the upper-class women began to gossip;

'The wife of the great lord has tried to seduce her slave.'

'She has such a passion for him.'

'She is clearly going astray.'

The rumours grew more and more exaggerated and distorted. When Zulaikha heard of this malicious talk she was very upset. How could the women of the city have any idea of the secret dream of her heart, or of the noble beauty of Joseph?

If only they could see how handsome Joseph is, they would not blame me, she thought. To justify herself in the eyes of these women, Zulaikha made a plan; first she would invite all the society ladies to a grand banquet.

In the banqueting hall the ladies reclined on silk cushions. They had drunk many glasses of wine and now they relaxed, at ease after such a splendid meal.

They whispered and gossiped about their hostess and the rumours that were spreading about her love for her slave.

The dessert was being served and each of them had a knife to peel the fruit when Zulaikha suddenly announced, 'Ladies, I have a surprise for you!' The door was flung open and Joseph walked into their midst. Immediately there was a flutter of surprise and delight as all the ladies turned to look at him. So distracted were they by his beauty that they cut their hands without realising what they were doing.

'How beautiful he is!' they exclaimed, 'God preserve us; he can't be a man, he must be a noble angel!'

Zulaikha was triumphant.

'This is Joseph, the man you blame me for! Would you not have reacted in the same way as I did? See, you have lost control of yourselves to such an extent that you have cut your hands! I did try to seduce him, but he rejected me.'

She paused, furious with Joseph for rejecting her. Seeking the support of the other women, she continued. 'But now, if he does not do as I say, I shall have him thrown into prison. Let us see if he will change his mind when he has to exchange the luxury of the palace for a dark prison cell!'

Joseph called upon God, 'O my Lord! I would prefer prison to what these women are inviting me to do. And if You don't avert their guile from me, I may yield to them and so become one of the ignorant.'

So, his Lord answered him and warded off their evil planning, as He is All-Knowing and All-Hearing.

Joseph knew that as a human being he was weak and that without the help of God, he would not have been able to resist this new attack on his virtue. Zulaikha's ruse had revealed that she was not alone in her fascination of Joseph and her desire to seduce him. They all thought that the threat of prison would be enough to weaken Joseph, but God gave him the Strength to prefer prison to a life of corruption at court.

The lord and all the noblemen of the court also thought that Joseph, although innocent, would have to be imprisoned if they were ever to restore order to their households. Joseph had caused such chaos among the women that the only solution seemed to be to remove him from society for a while.

How many young men today are willing to remain pure and chaste until they get married? It is no wonder that Joseph is the role model of purity and chastity among men. Similarly, Mary, the mother of Jesus, is the role model of purity and chastity among women.

Act IV: The Prison

So it was that Joseph, although guilty of no crime, was sent to prison. The people at court all had their own reasons for putting him there. But beyond their limited view, God was putting into effect His universal plan. The injustice of the lord and the plotting of the women would nevertheless lead to goodness and mercy. The prison cell brought back unpleasant memories of the time Joseph had spent in the well: the cold and dank stone walls, the dim light.

Joseph shivered, but he felt no bitterness at this new turn of events. He remembered how God was with him then; surely, He was with him now.

Two men were sent to prison at about the same time as Joseph. Both were court officials who were in disgrace. One was the chief steward, whose duty was to prepare the King's wines and drinks; the other was a baker who prepared the King's bread. In prison, they both had vivid dreams which puzzled them. Seeing that Joseph was wise, that he was kind and honest and would use his wisdom to help even strangers, they asked him for the meanings of these dreams.

One, whose dream had given him a feeling of hope, said, 'In my dream I saw myself pressing grapes for wine.'

The other, whose dream filled him with apprehension, said, I was carrying bread on my head and the birds were eating from it.

'Could you tell us the meaning of these dreams?', they asked, 'We see that you are a wise man who does good to all.'

Joseph replied, 'God has given me the ability to help you and very soon, before we have our next meal, be sure I will tell you the meaning of your dreams; but first let me tell you about my belief in God. I have abandoned the ways of the people around me who do not believe in God and even deny that there is life after death. I follow the path of my forefathers - Abraham, Isaac and Jacob. God has taught us never to attribute partners to Him, just as He has taught all mankind. But people have turned away from this Truth and have invented many gods. I speak to you as one prisoner to another: How could anyone believe that many lords, all fighting among themselves, could be better than the One True God? The gods you name are nothing but your inventions, without any reality behind them. The only reality is God; authority can only come through Him. He has commanded us to worship Him alone and no other. If people reject Him, then it is they who will suffer through their own fault. Believe in the One God and you will be successful in this life and in the life after death. This is your only true hope.'

Only after he had explained to them these important truths, which would give them comfort and support whatever their fate might be, did Joseph answer their questions about their dreams.

'Fellow prisoners, the one who dreamt about pressing grapes for wine will once more pour out the wine for his master. The other, unfortunate man will hang from the cross and the birds of the air will eat from his head. The matter about which you have been seeking my opinion has been so decreed.'

Then he said to the one who would be released from prison, 'Mention me to the King when you return to the court.'

Joseph felt that he had spent long enough in prison; how could he carry out all that God wanted him to do while he was cast off in a cell? A few days later, as Joseph had foretold, the steward left the prison, but he was so overjoyed at regaining his freedom and the comfort of his old lifestyle that Satan made the steward forget the suffering of Joseph.

Then, one day, the King called the Council of his advisers together to relate to them a dream which he could not understand and which was preying on his mind.

'I saw a vision of seven fat cows being devoured by seven thin cows, and there were seven green ears of corn and seven withered ears. Is there anyone who can tell me the meaning of this dream?'

No one wanted to take the responsibility of interpreting the dream, so the councillors replied
'We do not know how to interpret dreams, these are just nightmares.'

But suddenly the steward's conscience was awakened. He remembered Joseph still in prison, and remembered how skilled he was in the interpretation of dreams. He also thought that he might get some credit himself for satisfying the King's request, so instead of mentioning Joseph immediately, he asked for time to go away and reflect upon the meaning of the dream.

Straightaway he went to the prison and spoke to Joseph.

'O Joseph!' he said, 'O man of truth! The King has had a dream and no one can tell him the meaning of it.' He then recounted how the seven lean cows had devoured the seven fat cows and how there were seven withered ears of corn and seven green ears.'

To his surprise, Joseph did not reproach him for having forgotten him for so long in prison but simply gave him the interpretation of the dream.

'For seven years you must cultivate the land diligently and from the harvest you should take a little for the people to eat and store the rest. After this, there will be seven years of famine, during which time the stored grain can be used to feed the people; but you must keep a little for seed to sow when the famine is ended. After the drought will come a year in which there will be abundant water and you will press wine and oil once again.'

The steward hurried back to the King to give him this interpretation and to inform him of Joseph. Of course, the King wanted to see Joseph for himself and immediately sent a messenger to fetch him. The messenger expected Joseph to be overjoyed at this summons to appear at court, but first Joseph wanted to be sure that he was not returning to the same toxic environment that he had left behind.

'Go back to your lord and ask him of the ladies who cut their hands, and what their intention was. My Lord knows well their guile', Joseph said to the King's messenger.

Joseph did not know if the King was aware of all the mischief that had gone on, and he needed to be free from the persecution of these ladies if he was to accomplish the task that God had destined for him. He was careful not to mention Zulaikha who, after all, had been kind to him and who was young and immature when she tried to attract him.

The messenger conveyed this message to the King, who sent for the ladies; Zulaikha also came with them.

'What was this affair about?' he asked. 'Tell me the whole truth.' Reluctantly the women admitted that Joseph had done nothing wrong.

Then Zulaikha spoke. 'I will tell you the whole truth. Joseph is completely innocent. It was I who tried to seduce him. I take the blame entirely on myself!'

During the long years when Joseph had been in prison, Zulaikha had suffered a great deal and her lust for him had changed into a true and selfless love. She had been inspired by the example of Joseph, calm and patient in every turn of fortune. Her husband, the old lord, was now dead; perhaps now, in spite of her sin, she could be worthy of Joseph.

She continued, 'I say this so that Joseph may know that I have never plotted against him or been false to him in his absence. I realise that God will never allow such evil plans to succeed. I do not say that I am blameless. Human beings are so easily inclined to evil unless God, through His mercy, helps them to be good. And surely God forgives and is All-Merciful.'

Now that Joseph's innocence, wisdom, truthfulness and trustworthiness had been proven and confirmed before all the court, the King sent for him.

'You have been treated most unfairly', he said. 'Because of your honesty and wisdom, I should like to appoint you to a high position in the court. What post can I offer you?'

'Thanks be to God that the truth has been revealed!' exclaimed Joseph. 'There are hard years ahead for the whole country. I should be honoured if you would put me in charge of the granaries and storehouses of the land. I will look after them and see that there are enough supplies to last through the years of famine! I have knowledge and I'm trustworthy!

These credentials of possessing knowledge and being trustworthy further established Joseph in the land. He was not interested in living a life of idle luxury; rather, he took on the most difficult task in order to help the people.

And so it was that this youth who had been left for dead at the bottom of a cold, dark well, who had been sold into slavery for a handful of coins by his jealous brothers, who had later been unjustly accused and imprisoned, was now a chief minister in the most magnificent empire of the day.

In this way God provided an example for everyone, then and now, of goodness and faith; of purity and selflessness; of patience in adversity and trust in God. Joseph's faith had never faltered and his goodness was now rewarded, as God always rewards the efforts of those who persevere patiently and do good deeds. But Joseph knew that even better than the reward in this life is the reward with God in the life after death.

Act V: The Famine

Joseph, guided by God's wisdom and knowledge, directed the preparations for the predicted famine. The times of prosperity went by. The years of drought then came as foreseen, devastating both Egypt and its neighbouring countries alike. But Joseph had planned well and Egypt had enough corn to supply the people and even to sell to those who came from other starving lands. All were treated with courtesy and sold a carefully measured quota of grain.

With all this responsibility, Joseph never forgot his father and his brother, Benjamin. Would they have enough to eat in these difficult times? Would the other brothers persecute Benjamin as they had persecuted him? Then, one day, driven by the famine in their own country, the ten brothers arrived in Egypt to buy corn and came face to face with their long-lost brother.

They did not recognize Joseph; all they saw was a high-ranking Egyptian official, dressed in the Egyptian way, surrounded by his servants and staff. But Joseph immediately recognized them and without revealing his identity, entered into conversation with them. How long had they been travelling? Where was their father and why had he not come with them? Had they left any other brothers at home with their old father?

Once he started them talking about Benjamin, Joseph said, 'You must bring him with you next time. I should like to see him.'

The brothers were very reluctant to agree to this, but Joseph was insistent. 'You see how well I am treating you here; bring your stepbrother next time, or I shall give orders that you receive no more corn from Egypt.'

If the brothers were puzzled by the concern of this great court official for their brother Benjamin, they did not show it. They were only too anxious to be given permission to return for more grain when their current supply was exhausted. So, they said, 'We shall certainly ask our father if we can bring him next time, if that is what you wish.'

To encourage them to come again, Joseph ordered his servants to put back secretly into his brothers' saddlebags the goods they had brought with them to exchange for the corn. This way, they would be able to bring the same goods back with them to exchange for more food on their next journey.

When the brothers returned home they told Jacob all that had happened.

'We will not be given any more corn unless we return with our brother, Benjamin,' they said, 'so please send him with us so that we can buy more food. We will take good care of him.'

It was no easy task to persuade Jacob to let them take Benjamin; Jacob did not trust them at all after the loss of Joseph. 'Why should I trust you with him, when I trusted you with his brother before?' he said. 'But God is the best to take care of him and He is the most Merciful' Jacob knew that, whatever happened, only God could protect his son.

Then, when the brothers opened their baggage, imagine their surprise when they found that their goods had been returned to them. 'Look, father!' they exclaimed. 'Our goods have been sent back with us. Now we can take them again and get more food for our families. But we must take Benjamin with us. Do let him come! We shall take good care of him and return with an extra camel laden with provisions!'

At last Jacob replied, 'I will never send him with you unless you swear a solemn oath, in God's name, that you will bring him safely back to me unless you yourselves are prevented from returning.'

The brothers agreed and, when they had sworn their solemn oath, Jacob said, 'Over all that we say, May God be our Witness and our Guardian!'

Then, hoping to lessen the danger to his sons, he gave them some practical advice. 'My sons, when you enter the city, do not all go in by the same gate. Rather, all of you should enter from different gates. But no matter what advice I give you, only God can protect you. Above all put your trust in Him'

So, the brothers did as their kind and caring father said, but this human attempt to ward off danger did not in any way prevent God's plan from being carried out.

Now once more the brothers came into the presence of Joseph. He received them hospitably, even more so than he had done before and he asked the brothers if they had brought Benjamin with them. He then invited them to dine with him that evening and Joseph saw to it that Benjamin sat next to him. He made arrangements for them to stay in various houses but invited Benjamin to stay in his own palatial quarters. Thus, Joseph and Benjamin were able to spend some time alone together.

As soon as the other brothers had left, Joseph turned to Benjamin and said, 'I am your brother Joseph. Do not be upset at the way your brothers have been treating you.'

Benjamin stared in disbelief. Was this really his missing brother? This man was a government official at the court of Egypt. How did he come this far? Joseph explained everything and told him that he now had a plan and, whatever strange things happened, Benjamin was to keep silent.

The next day, when the brothers had collected their corn to take home, Joseph secretly hid the King's silver measuring cup in Benjamin's saddlebag. Then, just as they were slowly making their way out of the city there came a shout from one of the guards at the city gates.

'You in the caravan! Stop!' The brothers, turning in astonishment, inquired, 'What's happened? Why are you stopping us?'

'The King's silver cup is missing. You must have stolen it. We have to check your baggage. There is a reward of a camel-load of corn for anyone who will find it and I'm in charge of this.' The guard's face was dark with anger.

The brothers protested, 'We did not come here to make trouble. We are not thieves. There must be some mistake.'

'That may be, but we have orders to search you and if you are guilty, then what do you think your punishment should be?'

The brothers thought they had no reason to be afraid; they knew they had not stolen anything, so they replied boldly, 'If the cup is found in any of the saddlebags then the one to whom the saddlebag belongs should be held as a slave to pay for the crime. This is the way we punish those who do wrong.'

So began the search of their baggage, and because this was a very serious and important affair, Joseph personally conducted the whole operation. To make the search look convincing every item of baggage was examined, leaving Benjamin's till the end. Eventually there was a cry of triumph and the cup was held aloft.

This was not a wicked plan on the part of Joseph to plant stolen property on an innocent man. On the contrary, it is here that we can see the beauty and intricacy of God's plan; though in Egypt, the law of Canaan, with regard to thievery, was established for this particular case of the missing silver cup. In this way, Joseph and Benjamin were to be reunited under the pretence of Benjamin having to remain in Egypt to pay for his 'crime' of stealing. This false accusation against Benjamin, therefore, was part of God's plan to bring Joseph and his family together again, to bring comfort to Jacob in his old age and to bring about forgiveness and reconciliation. Human beings may plot and plan, but God sees everything. In His universal plan human wisdom, like that of Joseph's, plays a role in undoing the evil plots of men to bring about good to all; what is apparently wicked actually achieves goodness in the long-term.

The brothers, of course, were unaware of this and were eager to distance themselves from this crime.

'We are not surprised that this cup has turned up in Benjamin's luggage. His other brother Joseph used to steal too!'

Instead of defending their innocent brother Benjamin, the evil in their hearts was exposed through their reference to a crime that Joseph never committed. If only they had known that it was Joseph himself standing before them and that their lies and treachery would soon be exposed!

Joseph, his face showing no emotion, thought to himself, 'you have really made matters bad for yourselves now. Your crime is worse than stealing. God knows well that you are lying.'

The brothers were afraid of their father's anger. 'O exalted one, they pleaded, 'He has a father, a very old man, who will grieve for him. Take one of us in his place. We know you are a compassionate man.'

Joseph, however, was adamant. 'God forbid that we should take anyone other than the person on whom we found our property. In that case we would be acting wrongfully.'

When they saw that he would not change his mind, they held a conference, in private. The leader among them said, 'We all made a promise to our father in God's name that we would return with Benjamin. We have already once failed to keep our promise to look after Joseph; therefore, I will not leave this land until my father permits me or God commands me.'

The brothers listened attentively. The leader continued, 'Go back to your father and say that Benjamin has committed a theft without our knowledge. We could not have prevented something we knew nothing about.'

Could this be the same brother who suggested that Joseph should not be killed but be pushed into a well?

Perhaps he was different from the others! His sense of honour prevented him from going back to face his father, before whom he had already been proven inept and guilty in failing to safeguard Joseph.

The nine remaining brothers returned home and broke the news to their father as they had been instructed to do. They asked him to check their story with the people of the city where they had lodged and the caravan with which they had returned, in case their father still did not believe them.

Jacob was completely devastated by the story. He knew Benjamin too well to believe that he had committed a theft. He could not, would not believe it.

'No, this is a story you have made up between you. But I must be patient. Maybe God will return all of them to me at the end, for He is full of wisdom and knowledge.'

Once again Jacob, as a man of God, did not reprimand his sons or kick them out of his life. He did not take his revenge on them. Instead, he submitted to the will of God and accepted His trial. He chose to be patient, maintaining his faith in God and in Benjamin's innocence, without complaining to anyone regarding his anguish and sorrow. Jacob hoped that one day his children would ward off evil, mend their lives and be good to avert God's wrath. He conducted himself in the same manner as he did when he was told that the wolf devoured Joseph. In fact, the shock of this new loss of Benjamin brought back all the old grief over the disappearance of Joseph. This double grief was such that his eyes became white with sorrow, the light of the outside world became dim and blurred as darkness covered everything. Jacob's grief had made him blind and, unable to share his sorrow, he fell into a deep and uncomplaining melancholy.

The brothers became exasperated; they had no respect for their father in his old age, nor did they have any sympathy for his grief.

'Will you never stop thinking about Joseph!' they exclaimed.

Almost to himself, Jacob murmured, 'I only complain of my distress and anguish to God, and I know from God that which you do not know.' With this hope guiding him, Jacob sent his sons back to Egypt.

'My sons, go back, and enquire about Joseph and Benjamin. Never stop believing in God's soothing mercy. No one despairs of God's soothing mercy except those who have no faith.'

So, the brothers set off once more for Egypt. When they arrived, they rushed to see Joseph; they must tell him of their father's pain and sorrow. They also wanted to plead with him to be charitable and give them more grain, even though they had brought almost nothing with them in exchange.

'O exalted one', they said. 'Our father is suffering. He has lost his sight since Benjamin has been detained and, what is more, after all these years he has asked us to look for Benjamin's brother Joseph. We have brought very little to trade with, but we beg you to give us full measure as a gesture of charity; for God rewards the charitable.'

Joseph was moved to tears by the news of his father, and he said, 'You know how unjustly you treated Joseph and his brother, not knowing fully what you were doing?'

The brothers were startled to hear this. How did this Egyptian minister know all this?

Then one of them looked closely at the man standing before them in all his finery and suddenly recognising him, cried out, 'You are Joseph!'

'Yes, I am Joseph and this is my brother, Benjamin. We have suffered much but God has been gracious to us. He who is virtuous and patient is always rewarded by God.'

All that had been confusing for the ten brothers now became clear: the questions about the family in Canaan, the desire to see Benjamin and the inexplicable way that a silver cup had turned up in Benjamin's saddlebag. Surely the hand of God was to be seen behind all these events. Even Joseph's childhood dream was gradually becoming clear.

'Indeed, God has preferred you above all of us', the brothers said with realisation. 'And, certainly we have been guilty of sin.'

Joseph was glad that they had at last seen how wrong they were and that they were truly sorry for what they had done, but he did not want to spoil this moment of reconciliation. Besides, he wanted to send a message quickly to his father, telling him that all was well. He could not bear to think of him blind and suffering alone in Canaan.

'Don't reproach yourselves,' he said to his brothers. 'God will forgive you everything and I too forgive you.

Take my shirt to my father and put it on his face; then he will see again. Then come here together with all your families.'

Act VI: The Fulfilment of the Dream

Jacob, far away in Canaan, knew nothing of these developments. But even as the caravan left Egypt, he sensed deep in his soul the presence of the living Joseph. When he told the people around him, they laughed at him thinking he was an old man whose mind was wandering.

Then, when the brothers returned to Canaan, a bearer of the good news from among them ran to cast the shirt over

Jacob's face. The eyes which had grown dim with sadness could suddenly see again. Jacob was overjoyed; his faith had been rewarded.

'Did I not tell you that I know from God things that you do not know?' He said to his sons. They had not believed him when he had said this before, when everything seemed black, but now they came to see that he was right.

'O father, ask God to forgive us our sins', they pleaded.' For what we have done was very wrong.'

'I shall ask my Lord for forgiveness for you,' replied their father, 'For He is Oft-Forgiving and All-Merciful.'

The whole family, including Rachel's sister Leah, who had been like a mother to Joseph after the death of Rachel and was now married to his father Jacob, now set off for Egypt to be reunited with Joseph.

When they came into the presence of Joseph, he drew his parents to him and said, 'Enter Egypt in peace and security, by God's will.'

He welcomed them all by entertaining them and providing them with homes. He treated his father Jacob and his stepmother Leah with special dignity, seating them as guests of honour on a raised platform-like throne.

They in turn, parents and brothers alike, bowed down before Joseph in recognition of his high rank in Egypt under the King.

When he saw this, Joseph exclaimed, 'Father, this is the fulfilment of my dream I had long ago, when the sun, the moon and eleven stars bowed down before me. God has made it come true. God has been good to me. He took me out of prison and brought you all out of the desert to be with me here. It was Satan who misled my brothers and set them against me. Now God has made everything good. My Lord is the most Gracious and Merciful in achieving what He wills. He is All Knowing, and Truly Wise.'

So, Joseph, with a sound and pure heart, did not directly blame his brothers but instead blamed Satan for seducing and misleading them.

Joseph then prayed, 'O my Lord, it is You who have given me the power to interpret dreams and visions. Creator of the heavens and the earth, only You are the One I rely on in this world and the Hereafter. May I remain faithful to You always and when You take my soul at death, take it as the soul of a man who submitted himself absolutely to Your Will, and unite me with all who are virtuous.'

That was the painful journey which Jacob had to travel to get the dream of his beloved son Joseph to be fulfilled and to save the rest of his children. It was his patience and faith in God's mercy that healed the wounds of jealousy and hatred that had been inflicted on this family. As parents, are we willing to go as far as Jacob, in order to save our own families in this life and the hereafter?

Chapter Three - Moses, the Saviour of Israel

Moses' upbringing

The upbringing of Moses, in ancient Egypt, is mentioned in several chapters in the Holy Qur'an. However, I have only chosen Verses 1-28, from chapter 28. These Verses explain how God saved him from being killed by Pharaoh and the tests and trials he had to go through until he was chosen by God to save the Children of Israel from Pharaoh and his chiefs.

Given below are Verses 28:1-28 and the relevant footnotes.

(28:1): "Ta. Sin. Mim." (3326)
See n. 3137 to 26:1. FN3326

(28:2): "These are Verses of the Book that make (things) clear." (3327)
See n. 3138 to 26:2. FN3327

(28:3): "We rehearse to you (Muhammad) some of the story of Moses and Pharaoh in Truth, for people who believe." (3328)

"The part of the story of Moses told here is how Moses and his mother were guided in the child's infancy, that even as he grew up, he might be prepared for his high destiny; how in youth he trusted God in the most awkward situations and sought his help; how he fled into exile, and yet found

love and support because of his well-doing; and how,
when he was called to his mission, he received God's
favour, which defeated all the plots of his enemies. Thus,
God's Plan works continuously in the web of events. Those
who have faith will thus see the hand of God in everything
and welcome the light that comes to them by Revelation.
With such a Faith there is no room for Chance or blind
Fate." FN3328

**(28:4): "Truly Pharaoh elated himself in the land and
broke up its people into sections, (3329) depressing a
small group among them: their sons he slew, but he
kept alive their females: for he was indeed a maker of
mischief."**

"For a king or ruler to make invidious distinctions between
his subjects, and especially to depress or oppress any
particular class of his subjects, is a dereliction of his kingly
duties, for which he is responsible to God. Pharaoh and his
clique were intoxicated with pride of race and pride of
material civilization, and grievously oppressed the
Israelites. Pharaoh decreed that all sons born to his
Israelite subjects should be killed, and the females kept
alive for the pleasure of the Egyptians. Moses was saved
in a wonderful way, as related further." FN3329

**(28:5): "And We wished to be Gracious to those who
were being depressed on the land. (3330) To make
them leaders (in Faith) and make them heirs"**

"What Pharaoh wished was to crush them. But God's Plan
was to protect them as they were weak and indeed to
make them custodians and leaders in His Faith, and to
give them in inheritance a land 'flowing with milk and

honey'. Here they were established in authority for such time as they followed God's Law. As regards Pharaoh and his ministers and hosts, they were to be shown that they would suffer, at the hands of the Israelites, the very calamities against which they were so confidently taking precautions for themselves." FN3330

(28:6): "To establish a firm place for them in the land, and to show Pharaoh, Haman, (3331) and their hosts, at their hands, the very things against which they were taking precautions." (3332)

"Haman was evidently Pharaoh's minister, not to be confounded with a Haman who is mentioned in the Old Testament (Esther 3:1), as a minister of Ahasuerus (Xerxes) King of Persia, the same who invaded Greece, and ruled from B.C. 485 to 464." FN3331

"Pharaoh was trying to kill the Israelites. Instead, the Plagues of Egypt, invoked by Moses, killed thousands of Egyptians (7:133. and notes 1091-92), because 'they were steeped in arrogance, a people given to sin.' In pursuing the Israelites in their flight, Pharaoh and his army were themselves overwhelmed in the sea." FN3332

(28:7): "So We sent this inspiration to the mother of Moses: 'Suckle (your child), but when you have fears about him, cast him into the river, (3333) but fear not nor grieve: for We shall restore him to you, and We shall make him one of Our messengers.'"

"The Egyptian midwives had orders to kill Israelite babies. Moses was saved from them, and his mother nursed the infant at her breast herself. But when the danger of

discovery was imminent, she put him into a chest or basket, and floated him on the river Nile. It flowed by the King's palace, and the chest with the baby was picked up, as related further on. The mother had no cause to fear or grieve afterwards, as the child grew up under her tender care and became afterwards one of the Prophets of God." FN3333

(28:8): "Then the people of Pharaoh picked him up (from the river): (It was intended) that (Moses) should be to them an adversary and a cause of sorrow:(3334) for Pharaoh and Haman and (all) their hosts were men of sin."

"This was the Plan of Providence; that the wicked might cast a net round themselves by fostering the man who was to bring them to naught and be the instrument of their punishment-or (looking at it from the other side) that Moses might learn all the wisdom of the Egyptians in order to expose all that was hollow and wicked in it."FN3334

(28:9): "The wife of Pharaoh said: '(Here is) joy of the eye, (3335) for me and for you: slay him not. It may be that he will be of use to us, or we may adopt him as a son.' And they perceived not (what they were doing)!" (3336)

"He was a darling to look at, and Pharaoh had apparently no son, but only a daughter, who afterwards shared his throne. This is on the supposition that the Pharaoh was Thothmes I (see Appendix IV, S. 7)." FN3335

"In all life Providence so orders things that Evil is defeated by its own weapons. Not only is it defeated, but it actually, *though unwittingly, advances the cause of Good! In non-religious language this is called the work of the Ironic Fates. If Thomas Hardy had not made Napoleon the Puppet of Fate in his 'Dynasts', he could well have taken Pharaoh as an illustration of the Irony of Fate, or, as we should prefer to call it, the working of the Universal Plan of God." FN3336*

(28:10): "But there came to be a void in the heart of the mother of Moses: She was going almost to disclose his (case), had We not strengthened her heart (with faith), so that she might remain a (firm) believer." (3337)

"The mother's heart felt the gaping void at parting from her son; but her Faith in God's Providence kept her from betraying herself." FN3337

(28:11): "And she said to the sister of (Moses), "Follow him" so she (the sister) watched him in the character of a stranger. And they knew not."

(28:12): "And we ordained that he refused to suck at first, until (His sister came up and) said: 'Shall I point out to you the people of a house that will nourish and bring him up for you (3338) and be sincerely attached to him?'"

"For you: i.e., on your behalf. Thus, Moses got the benefit of his mother's milk (symbolical of all the traditions and spiritual heritage of his ancestry and his people) as well as the prestige and the opportunities of being brought up in the royal family, with the best of teachers to teach him

Egyptian wisdom. In addition, there was the comfort to his mother." FN3338

(28:13): "Thus, did We restore him to his mother, that her eye might be comforted, that she might not grieve, and that she might know that the promise of God is true: but most of them do not understand." (3339)

"God's promise is always true, but short-sighted people, if they are a little thwarted in their plan, do not understand that God's wisdom, power, and goodness are far more comprehensive than any little plans which they may form." FN3339

(28:14): "When he reached full age, and was firmly established (3340) (in life), We bestowed on him wisdom and knowledge: for thus do We reward those who do good."

"Full age may be taken to be mature youth, say between 18 and 30 years of age. By that time a person is fully established in life: his physical build is completed, and his mental and moral habits are formed. In this case, as Moses was good at heart, true and loyal to his people, and obedient and just to those among whom he lived. He was granted wisdom and knowledge from on high, to be used for the times of conflict which were coming for him. His internal development being complete, he now goes out into the outer world, where he is again tried and proved, until he gets his divine commission." FN3340

(28:15): "And he entered the city at a time when its people (3341) were not watching: and he found there two men fighting, - one of his own religion, and the

other, of his foes. Now the man of his own religion appealed to him against his foe, and Moses struck (3342) him with his fist and made an end of him. He said: 'This is a work of Evil (Satan): "for he is an enemy that manifestly misleads!"'

"That may have been either the time of the noontide siesta, when all business is suspended even now in Egypt, or the time of night, when people are usually asleep. The latter is more probable, in view of verse 18 below. But there is also another suggestion. A guest in a Palace is not free to wander about at will in the plebeian quarters of the City at all sorts of hours, and this applies even more to an inmate of the Palace brought up as a son. Moses was therefore visiting the City privately and eluding the guards. His object may have been to see for himself how things were going on; perhaps he had heard that his people were being oppressed, as we may suppose that he had retained contact with his mother." FN3341

"His object was apparently to strike him so as to release the Israelite, not to kill the Egyptian. In fact, he killed the Egyptian. This was unfortunate in more ways than one. His visit to the City was clandestine; he had taken the side of the weaker and despised party; and he had taken the life of an Egyptian. He was full of regrets and repentance, and he prayed to God, and obtained God's forgiveness." FN3342

(28:16): "He prayed: 'O my Lord! I have indeed wronged my soul! Do You then forgive me!' So (God) forgave him: for He is the Oft-Forgiving, Most Merciful."

(28:17): "He said: 'O my Lord! For that You have bestowed Your Grace on me, never shall I be a help to those who sin!'" (3343)

"He takes a conscious and solemn vow to dedicate himself to God, and to do nothing that may in any way assist those who were doing wrong. This was his general idea, but no plan had yet shaped itself in his mind, until a second catastrophe brought matters to a head, and he was plunged in adventure." FN3343

(28:18): "So, he saw the morning in the city, looking about, in a state of fear, when behold, the man who had, the day before, sought his help called aloud for his help (again). Moses said to him: 'You are truly, it is clear, a quarrelsome fellow!'" (3344)

"The man was an Israelite. But Moses was himself in a distracted mood, for the reasons given in FN3342 above, and he was exasperated at this public appeal to him again." FN3344

(28:19): "Then, when he decided to lay hold of the man who was (3345) an enemy to both of them, that man said: 'O Moses! Is it your intention to slay me as you slewed a man yesterday? Your intention is none other than to become a powerful violent man in the land, and not to be one who sets things right!'" (3346)

"When Moses considered further that the Egyptian was unjust and that the Egyptian was an enemy to Israel generally (including both Moses and the man assaulted), he was going to intervene again, when he received a double warning, one from the Egyptian who was fighting,

and the other from some man (Israelite or Egyptian) who was friendly to him, as explained below. We may suppose that after the first day's fight, there had been a great deal of talk in the bazaars, both among Israelites and Egyptians. Probably, the Israelites were elated at finding a champion-perhaps more elated than they should have been, and in a provocative mood, which deserved Moses' rebuke. Probably the Egyptians had discussed who this new champion was, and had already appraised the Palace, to which Moses had not dared to return." FN3345

"The Egyptian saw the tactical advantage of his position. In effect he said: 'We have found out all about you. You live in the Palace, and yet you come clandestinely and kill our Egyptians. Are you going to do the same with me? You are nothing but a bully! And you talk of setting things right! That is what you should do if you were true to your salt!' FN3346

(28:20): "And there came a man, running, from the furthest end (3347) of the City. He said: 'O Moses! the Chiefs are taking counsel together about you, to slay you, so get away, for I do give you sincere advice.'"

"Apparently rumours had reached the Palace, a Council had been held, and the death of Moses had been decreed!" FN3347

(28:21): "He therefore got away therefrom, (3348) looking about, in a state of fear. He prayed 'O my Lord! save me from people given to wrong-doing.'"

"Moses saw that his position was now untenable, both in the Palace and in the City, and indeed anywhere in

Pharaoh's territory. So he suffered voluntary exile. But he did not know where to go to. His mind was in a state of agitation. But he turned to God and prayed. He got consolation, and felt that after all it was no hardship to leave Egypt, where there was so much injustice and oppression." FN3348

(28:22): "Then, when he turned his face towards (the land of) Madyan, (3349) he said: 'I do hope that my Lord will show me the smooth and straight Path.'"

"East of Lower Egypt, for about 300 miles, runs the Sinai Peninsula, bounded on the south by the Gulf of Suez, and on the north by what was the Isthmus of Suez, now cut by the Suez Canal . Over the Isthmus ran the high road to Palestine and Syria, but a fugitive could not well take that road, as the Egyptians were after him. If he could, after crossing the Isthmus, plunge into the Sinai desert, east or southeast, he would be in the Midianite territory, where the people would be Arabs and not Egyptians. He turned thither and again prayed to Allah for guidance." FN3349

(28:23): "And when he arrived at the watering (place) in Madyan,(3350) he found there a group of men watering (their flocks), and besides them he found two women who were keeping back (their flocks). He said: 'What is the matter with you?' They said: 'We cannot water (our flocks) until the shepherds take back (their flocks) And our father is a very old man.'" (3351)

"The first thing that a wanderer in a desert would make for would be an oasis where he could get water from a spring or well, the shade of trees against the scorching sun, and some human company. The Midianite watering place was

86

probably a deep well, as surface springs are rare in sandy desert, where the water level is low, unless there was a hill from which issued a spring" FN3350

"Here is a pretty, little idyll, told in the fewest and most beautiful words possible. Moses arrives, at an oasis in the desert, weary and travel-worn, with his mind full of anxiety and uncertainty owing to his recent experiences in Egypt. He was thirsty and would naturally seek water. At the well or spring he found shepherds (or perhaps goatherds) watering their flocks. As a stranger it was not for him to thrust himself among them. He waited under the shade of a tree until they should finish. He noticed two damsels, also waiting, with their flocks, which they had come to water. His chivalry was roused. He went at once among the goatherds, made a place for the flocks of the damsels, gave them water, and then resumed his place in the shade. They were modest maidens, and had given him in three Arabic words the key to the whole situation. 'Abuna shaykhun kabir' our father is a very old man, and therefore cannot come to water the flocks; we therefore do the work; we could not very well thrust ourselves among these men.'" FN3351

(28:24): "So, he watered (their flocks) for them; then he turned back to the shade and said: 'O my Lord! truly I am in (desperate) need of any good that You do send me!'" (3352)

"The maidens are gone, with smiles on their lips and gratitude in their hearts. What were the reflections of Moses as he returned to the shade of the tree? He returned thanks to Allah for the bright little vision which he had just seen. Had he done a good deed? Precious was

the opportunity he had had. He had slaked his thirst. But he was a homeless wanderer and had a longing in his soul, which he dared not put into words. Those shepherds were no company for him. He was truly like a beggar in desperate need. For any little good that came his way, he was grateful. But what was this? This vision of a comfortable household, presided over by an old man rich in flocks and herds, and richer still in two daughters, as modest as they were beautiful? Perhaps he would never see them again! But Providence was preparing another surprise for him." FN3352

(28:25): "Afterwards one of the (damsels) came (back) to him, walking bashfully. She said: 'My father invites you that he may reward you for having watered (3353) (our flocks) for us.' So when he came to him and narrated the story, he said: 'Fear you not: (well) you have been saved from the unjust people.'" (3354)

"Scarcely had he rested, when one of the damsels came back, walking with bashful grace! Modestly she gave her message, 'My father is grateful for what you did for us. He invites you, that he may thank you personally, and at least give some return for your kindness.'" FN3353

"Nothing could have been more welcome than such a message, and through such a messenger. Moses went, of course, and saw the old man. He found such a well-ordered patriarchal household. The old man was happy with his daughters and they with him. There was mutual confidence. They had evidently described the stranger to him in terms which made his welcome a foregone conclusion. On the other hand, Moses had allowed his imagination to paint the father in something of the glorious *colours in which his daughters had appeared to him like an angelic vision. The two men got to be friends at once. Moses told the old man his story - who he was, how he was brought up, and what misfortunes had made him quit Egypt. Perhaps the whole household, including the daughters, listened breathlessly to his tale. Perhaps their wonder and admiration were mingled with a certain amount of pity - perhaps with some more tender feeling in the case of the girl who had been to fetch him. Perhaps the enchantment which Desdemona felt in Othello's story was working on her. In any case the stranger had won his place in their hearts. The old man, the head of the household, assured him of hospitality and safety under his roof. As one with a long experience of life he congratulated him on his escape. 'Who would live among unjust people? It is as well you are free of them!'" FN3354*

(28:26): "Said one of the (damsels) 'O my (dear) father! Engage (3355) him on wages: truly the best of men for you to employ is the (man) who is strong and trusty'...." (3356)

"A little time passes. A guest, after all, cannot stay forever. They all felt that it would be good to have him with them permanently. The girl who had given her heart to him had spoken their unspoken thoughts. Why not employ him to tend the flocks? The father was old, and a young man was wanted to look after the flocks. And-there may be other possibilities." FN3355

"Strong and trusty: Moses had proved himself to be both, and these were the very qualities which a woman most admires in the man she loves." FN3356

(28:27): "He said: 'I intend to wed one of these my daughters to you, on condition that you serve me for eight years;(3357) but if you complete ten years, it will be (grace) from you. But I intend not to place you under a difficulty: you will find me, indeed, if God wills, one of the righteous.'"

"A little time passed, and at length the father broached the subject of marriage. It was not for the fugitive to suggest a permanent tie, especially when, in the wealth of this world, the girl's family was superior, and they had an established position, while he was a mere wanderer. The father asked if he would marry one of the daughters and stay with them for at least eight years, or if he liked, ten years, but the longer term was at his option. If he brought no dower, his service for that period was more than sufficient in lieu of dower. The particular girl intended was no doubt tacitly settled long before, by the mutual attraction of the young hearts themselves. Moses was glad of the proposal, and accepted it. They ratified it in the most solemn manner, by appealing to God. The old man, knowing the worth of his son-in-law, solemnly assured him that in any event he would not take advantage of his position to be a hard task-master or to insist on anything inconsistent with Moses's interests, should a new future open out to him. And a new and glorious future was awaiting him after his apprenticeship." FN3357

(28:28): "He said: 'Be that (the agreement) between me and you: whichever of the two terms I fulfil, let there be no ill-will to me. Be God a witness to what we say.'" (3358)

"In patriarchal society it was not uncommon to have a marriage bargain of this kind conditional on a certain term of service. In this case the episode conveys two lessons. (1) A man destined to be a messenger of Allah is yet a man, and must pass through the ups and downs of life like any other man: only he will do it with more grace and distinction than other men. (2) The beautiful relations in love and marriage may themselves be a preparation for the highest spiritual destiny that may await a Messenger of Allah. A woman need not necessarily be a snare and a temptation: she may be the understanding help-mate that the Lady Khadijah was to the Prophet Muhammad."
FN3358

Moses' first encounter with God

The first encounter between God and Moses occurred when God spoke directly to him on Mount Sinai in Egypt. God says at the end Verse

4:164:*"………. And God spoke to Moses directly."*

Moses was the only Messenger to whom God spoke directly without the involvement of ArchAngel Gabriel.

After completing the term he had agreed to with his father-in-law, Moses left his temporary residence in Midianite and embarked on a journey with his family towards Egypt. He could not imagine what was waiting for him when he saw a burning bush in the middle of the desert.

The encounter with God is mentioned in many chapters in the Qur'an, for example in Chapters 20:9-48, 26:10-17, 27:7-12, 28:29-35 and 79:15-19.

Although God, the Author, remains the same throughout the Qur'an, each chapter presents the story from a different perspective.

Firstly, I will give below the Verses and the footnotes from chapter 28 as they are the continuation from the previous section 3.1. After that I will give the relevant Verses from chapter 20 and the footnotes.

A) Chapter 28, Verses 29-35

(28:29): "Now when Moses had fulfilled the term, and was travelling (3359) with his family, he perceived a fire in the direction of Mount Tur. He said to his family: 'Wait here, I perceive a fire; I hope to bring you from there some information, or a burning firebrand, that you may warm yourselves.'" (3360)

" The episode in the desert, full of human interest, now closes, and we come to the threshold of the sacred Call to the divine ministry of Moses. Here we may compare this passage with that in 27:7-14 and previous passages. In this passage we are told, after reference to Moses's preparation for his high destiny, of the particular sin of Arrogance and Sacrilege of which Pharaoh was guilty (28:38-39), how it was punished, and with what instruments in the hands of Moses and Pharaoh. The notes on the earlier passage should be read, as

explanations already given need not now be repeated."
FN3359

"Note how the transition is effected from the happy earthly life of Moses (with its previous earthly storm and stress) to the new spiritual storm and stress of his prophetic mission." FN3360

(28:30): "But when he came to the (fire), a voice was heard from the right bank of the valley, from a tree (3361) in hallowed ground: 'O Moses! Verily I am God, the Lord of the Worlds.'"

"We are to suppose the appearance of a bush burning but not consumed (Exod. 3:2), a device adopted by the Scottish Church in its armorial bearings. Scotland apparently took that emblem and motto (Nes tamen consumebatur, 'nevertheless it was not consumed') from the Synod of the Reformed Church of France, which had adopted it in 1583. (I am indebted for this information to the Rev. D.Y. Robertson, Chaplain of the Church of Scotland in Simla, India). The real explanation of the Burning Bush will be found in 27:8. n. 3245: it was not a fire, but a reflection of the Glory of God." FN3361

(28:31): "'Now throw your rod!' but when he saw it moving (of its own accord) as if it had been a snake, he turned back in retreat, and retraced not his steps. 'O Moses!' (It was said), 'Draw near, and fear not: for you are of those who are secure.'" (3362)

"The verbal meaning is: 'you have nothing to fear from what appears to be a snake: it is a snake, not for you, but for Pharaoh.' But there is a deeper meaning besides.

Moses had now been called to a higher and spiritual mission. He had to meet the hatred of the Egyptians and circumvent their trickery and magic. He had now the security of Faith: in all dangers and difficulties God would guide and protect him, for he was actually in God's service, one of the Elect." FN3362

(28:32): "'Move your hand into your bosom, and it will come forth white without stain (or harm), and draw your hand close to your side (to guard) against fear. (3363) Those are the two credentials from your Lord to Pharaoh and his Chiefs: for truly they are a people rebellious and wicked.'"

"Literally, 'draw your wing close to your side, (away) from fear'. When a bird is frightened, it ruffles its wings and prepares to fly away, but when it is calm and composed, it sits with its wings drawn close to its sides, showing a mind secure from danger: Cf. also n. 2550 to 20:22." FN3363

(28:33): "He said: 'O my Lord! I have slain a man among them, and I fear (3364) lest they slay me."

"It is not that Moses is not reassured from all fear on account of the apparent snake which his rod had become, or from the sacred and unfamiliar surroundings in which he found himself. On this point his heart had been completely assured. But he is still new to his mission, and the future is obscure to his mind. Pharaoh was after him, to take his life, and apparently with good cause, because one of Pharaoh's men had been slain at his hands. And now he is commanded to go to Pharaoh and rebuke him and his Chiefs. The inner doubts and difficulties of his human mind he frankly lays before his Lord, and asks for a little human

94

and visible support, which is granted him at once, viz.: the help of his brother Aaron." FN3364

(28:34): "'And my brother Aaron - He is more eloquent in speech than I: so send him with me as a helper, to confirm (and strengthen) me: for I fear that they may accuse me of falsehood.'"

(28:35): "He said: 'We will certainly strengthen your arm through your brother, and invest you both with authority, so they shall not be able to (3365) touch you: with Our Sign you shall triumph,- you two as well as those who follow you.'" (3366)

"To touch you: to approach you anywhere near, in the wonders and Signs that you will show them under the divine authority with which you are invested." FN3365

"The potency of God's Light is such that its divine rays reach the humblest of those who seek after Him. The Prophets can certainly work wonders, but their sincere followers in Faith can do so also in their own spheres. Wonders may appeal to people, but they are not the highest Signs of God's workings and they are around us every day in our lives." FN3366

B) Chapter 20, Verses 9-48

(20:9): "Has the story of Moses (2540) reached you (O Muhammad)?"

"The story of Moses in its different incidents is told in many places in the Qur'an, and in each case the phase most appropriate in the context is referred to or emphasised. In 2:49-61, it was a phase from the religious history of mankind; in 7:103-162, it was a phase from the story of the 'Ummah (or nation) of Israel, and the story was continued to the times after Moses; in 17:101-103, we have a picture of the decline of a soul in the arrogance of Pharaoh; here, in 20:9-24, we have a picture of the rise of a soul in the commission given to Moses from God; in 20:25-36, we have his spiritual relationship with his brother Aaron; in 20:37-40, we have his spiritual relation with his mother and sister, and his upbringing; in 20:41-76, we have his spiritual combat with Pharaoh; and in 20:77-98, we have his spiritual combat with his own people, the Israelites. For other incidents, consult the Index." FN2540

(20:10): "Behold, he saw a fire:(2541) So he said to his family, "Wait here; I perceive a fire; perhaps I can bring you some burning brand therefrom, or find some guidance at the fire."(2542)

"A fire. It appeared like an ordinary fire, which always betokens the presence of men in a desert or a lonely place. Moses made for it alone, to fetch the wherewithal for making a fire for his family, and perhaps to find some direction as to the way, from the people he should meet there. But it was not an ordinary fire. It was a Burning Bush; a Sign of the Glory of God." FN2541

"The spiritual history of Moses begins here. It was his spiritual birth. His physical life, infancy, and upbringing are referred to later on, to illustrate another point. Moses, when he grew up, left the palace of Pharaoh and went to the Midianite people, in the Sinai peninsula . He married among them, and was now travelling with his family and his flocks, when he was called to his mission by God. He went to look for a fire for comfort and guidance. He found a higher and holier comfort and guidance. The whole passage is full of portent meaning, which is reflected in the short rhymed verses in the original." FN2542

(20:11): "But when he came to the fire, a voice was heard: 'O Moses!'"

(20:12): "Verily I am Your Lord! Therefore (in My presence) (2543) put off your shoes: you are in the sacred valley Tuwa." (2544)

"The shoes are to be put off as a mark of respect. Moses was now to put away his mere worldly interests, and anything of mere worldly utility, he having been chosen by God, the Most High." FN2543

"This was the valley just below Mount Sinai , where subsequently he was to receive the Law. In the parallel mystic meaning, we are selected by trials in this humble life, whose valley is just as sacred and receives Allah's glory just as much as the heights of the Mount Tur if we but have the insights to perceive it." FN2544

(20:13): "I have chosen you: listen, then, to the inspiration (sent to you)"

(20:14): "Verily, I am God. There is no god but I: So serve Me (only), and establish regular prayer for celebrating My praise."

(20:15): "Verily the Hour of Judgment is coming -(2545) My design is to keep it hidden -(2546) for every soul to receive its reward by the measure of its Endeavour."

"The first need is to mend our lives and worship and serve Allah, as in the last verse. The next is to realise the meaning of the Hereafter, when every soul will get the meed of its conduct in this life." FN2545

"Ukhfi may mean either "keep it hidden", or "make it manifest", and the Commentators have taken, someone meaning and some the other. If the first is taken, it means that the exact hour or day when the Judgement comes is hidden from man; if the second, it means that the fact of the Judgement to come is made known, that man may remember and take warning. I think that both meanings are implied." FN2546

(20:16): "Therefore let not such as believe not therein but follow their own lusts, divert you therefrom, (2547) lest you perish!"

"Moses had yet to meet the formidable opposition of the arrogant Pharaoh and his proud Egyptians, and later, the rebellion of his own people. In receiving his commission, he is warned of both dangers. This relates to man's own soul: when once the light reaches him let him hold fast to it, lest he perish. He will be beset with dangers of all kinds around him: the worst will be the danger of unbelieving

people who seem to thrive on their selfishness and in following their own vain desires!" FN2547

(20:17): "And what is that in your right hand, O Moses?"

(20:18): "He said, 'It Is (2548) my rod: on it I lean; with it I beat down fodder for my flocks; and in it I find other uses.'"

"Now comes the miracle of the rod. First of all, the attention of Moses himself is drawn to it, and he thinks of the ordinary uses to which he puts it in his daily life." FN2548

(20:19): "(God) said, 'Throw it, O Moses!'"

(20:20): "He threw it, and behold! It was a snake, active in motion" (2549)

"Cf. 7:107, where a different word (thu'ban is used for "snake", and the qualifying adjective is "plain (for all to see)". The scene there is before Pharaoh and his magicians and people: the object is to show the hollowness of their magic by a miracle: the rod appears before them as a long and creeping, writhing serpent. Here there is a symbol to present God's Mystery to Moses's mind and understanding: the rod becomes a Hayy (a live snake), and its active motion is what is most to be impressed on the mind of Moses, for there were no other spectators. So the highest spiritual mysteries can be grasped, with God's gift of insight, from the most ordinary things of daily use. Once they are grasped, there is no

question of fear. They really are the virtues of this life lifted up to the glorious spiritual plane." FN2549

(20:21): "(God) said, 'Seize it, and fear not: We shall return it at once to its former condition'"

(20:22): "Now draw your hand (2550) close to your side: It shall come forth white (and shining), without harm (or stain), - as another Sign"

"The second of the greater Miracles shown to Moses was the "White (shining) Hand". Ordinarily, when the skin becomes white, it is a sign of disease, leprosy or something loathsome. Here there was no question of disease: on the contrary, the hand was glorified, and it shone as with a divine light. Such a miracle was beyond Egyptian or human magic (Cf. 27:12 and 28:32). FN2550

(20:23): "In order that We may show you (two) of our Greater Signs."

(20:24): ""Go to Pharaoh, (2551) for he has indeed transgressed all bounds."

"Moses, having been spiritually prepared now gets his definite commission to go to Pharaoh and point out the error of his ways. So inordinate was Pharaoh's vanity that he had it in his mind to say: "I am your Lord Most High!" (79:24)." FN2551

(20:25): "(Moses) said: "O my Lord! Expand me my breast;"(2552)

"The breast is reputed to be the seat of knowledge and affections. The gift of the highest spiritual insight is what he prays for first. Cf. 94:1. This was the most urgent in point of time. There are three other things he also asks for: viz., (1) God's help in his task, which at first appears difficult to him; (2) the gift of eloquence, and the removal of the impediment from his speech; and (3) the counsel and constant attendance with him of his brother Aaron, whom he loved and trusted, for he would otherwise be alone among the Egyptians."FN2552

(20:26): ""Ease my task for me;"

(20:27): "And remove the impediment (2553) from my speech,"

"Literally, "Loosen a knot from my tongue"." FN2553

(20:28): "So they may understand what I say:"

(20:29): "And give me a Minister from my family,"

(20:30): "Aaron, my brother;"

(20:31): "Add to my strength (2554) through him,"

"Literally, "Strengthen my back with him". A man's strength lies in his back and backbone so that he can stand erect and boldly face his tasks." FN2554

(20:32): "And make him share my task:"
(20:33): "That we may celebrate (2555) Your praise without stint,"

"The requests that Moses makes are inspired, not by earthly but by spiritual motives. The motive, expressed in the most general terms, is to glorify Allah, not in an occasional way, but systematically and continuously, "without stint." The clauses in this verse and the next, taken together, govern all the requests he makes, from verse 25 to verse 32." FN2555

(20:34): "And remember You without stint:"

(20:35): "For You are He that (ever) regards us."(2556)

"The celebration of God's praise and remembrance is one form of showing gratitude on the part of Moses for the Grace which God had bestowed upon him." FN2556

(20:36): "(God) said: "Granted is your prayer, O Moses!"

(20:37): "And indeed We conferred a favour on you another time (before)."

(20:38): ""Behold! We sent (2557) to your mother, by inspiration, the message:"

"The story is not told, but only those salient points recapitulated which bear on the spiritual upbringing" and work of Moses. Long after the age of Joseph, who had been a Wazir to one of the kings, there came on the throne of Egypt a Pharaoh who hated the Israelites and wanted them annihilated. He ordered Israelite male children to be killed when they were born. Moses's mother hid him for a time, but when further concealment was impossible, a thought crossed her mind that she should put her child into

*a chest and send the chest floating down the Nile. This
was not merely a foolish fancy of hers. It was God's Plan to
bring up Moses in all the learning of the Egyptians, in order
that that learning itself should be used to expose what was
wrong in it and to advance the glory of God. The chest was
floated into the river Nile. It flowed on into a stream that
passed through Pharaoh's Garden. It was picked up by
Pharaoh's people and the child was adopted by Pharaoh's
wife. See 28:4-13." FN2557*

**(20:39): "´Throw (the child) into the chest, and throw
(the chest) into the river: the river will cast him up on
the bank, and he will be taken up by one who is an
enemy to Me and an enemy to him´:(2558) But I cast
(the garment of) love over you from Me:(2559) and
(this) in order that you may be reared under Mine eye"
(2560)**

*"Pharaoh was an enemy to God, because he was puffed
up and he blasphemed, claiming to be God himself. He
was an enemy to the child Moses, because he hated the
Israelites and wanted to have their male children killed;
also because Moses stood for God's revelation to come"
FN2558*

*"God made the child comely and lovable, and he attracted
the love of the people who, on general grounds, would
have killed him." FN2559*

*"See n. 2558 above. By making the child Moses so
attractive as to be adopted into Pharaoh's household, not
only was Moses brought up in the best way possible from
an earthly point of view, but God's special Providence
looked after him in bringing his mother to him, as stated in*

103

the next verse, and thus nourishing him on his mother's milk and keeping in touch, in his inner growth, with the feelings and sentiments of his people, the Israelites."
FN2560

(20:40): "Behold! Your sister goes forth and says, ´shall I show you one who will nurse and rear the (child)?' (2561) So We brought you back to your mother, that her eye (2562) might be cooled and she should not grieve. Then you did slay (2563) a man, but We saved you from trouble, and We tried you in various ways. Then you did tarry a number of years with the people of Midian. (2564) Then you did come hither as ordained, O Moses!"

"We may suppose that the anxious mother, after the child was floated on the water, sent the child's sister to follow the chest from the bank and see where and by whom it was picked up. When it was picked up by Pharaoh's own family and they seemed to love the child, she appeared like a stranger before them, and said, "Shall I search out a good wet nurse for the child, that she may rear the child you are going to adopt?" That was exactly what they wanted. She ran home and told her mother. The mother was delighted to come and fold the infant in her arms again and feed it at her own breast, and all openly and without any concealment." FN2561

"The mother's eyes had, we may imagine, been sore with scalding tears at the separation from her baby. Now they were cooled: a phrase meaning that her heart was comforted." FN2562

"Years passed. The child grew up. In outward learning he was of the house of Pharaoh. In his inner soul and sympathy he was of Israel. One day, he went to the Israelite colony and saw all the Egyptian oppression under which Israel laboured. He saw an Egyptian smiting an Israelite, apparently with impunity. Moses felt brotherly sympathy and smote the Egyptian. He did not intend to kill him, but in fact the Egyptian died of the blow. When this became known, his position in Pharaoh's household became impossible. So he fled out of Egypt, and was only saved by God's grace. He fled to the Sinai Peninsula, to the land of the Midianites, and had various adventures. He marries one of the daughters of the Midianite chief, and lived with the Midianites for many years, as an Egyptian stranger. He had many trials and temptations, but he retained his integrity of character." FN2563

"See last note. After many years spent in a quiet life, grazing his father-in-law's flocks, he came one day to the valley of Tuwa underneath the great mountain mass of Sinai, called Tur (in Arabic). The peak on the Arabian side (where Moses was) was called Horeb by the Hebrews. Then was fulfilled God's Plan: he saw the fire in the distance, and when he went up, he was addressed by God and chosen to be God's Messenger for that age." FN2564

(20:41): ""And I have prepared you for Myself (for service)."

(20:42): "Go, you and your brother. (2565) With My Signs, and don't slack, either of you, in keeping Me in remembrance."

"We may suppose that Moses had fled alone to the land of Midian, and that he had now come alone (with his family but not with his brother) to Tuwa, as described in FN2542 above. When he was honoured with his mission, and was granted his request that his brother Aaron should accompany him, we may suppose that he took steps to get Aaron to come to him, and their meeting was in Tuwa. Some time may be supposed to have elapsed before they were in Egypt, and then they prayed, and received these directions in their Egyptian home.Aaron was either an elder or a younger brother — we are not told which. In either case he was born when the ban on Israelite new-born babes was not in operation. Moses had been out of touch with him, and it speaks greatly for his family affection that he remembered him and prayed for his comradeship in the most serious spiritual work of his life." FN2565

(20:43): ""Go, both of you, to Pharaoh, (2566) for he has indeed transgressed all bounds;" (2567)

"Their mission was in the first instance to Pharaoh and to the Egyptians, and then to lead Israel out of Egypt." FN2566

"Compare the same phrase in 20:24. Having glanced at the early life of Moses we come back now to the time when Moses's actual ministry begins. The earlier personal story of Moses is rounded off." FN2567

(20:44): ""But speak to him mildly; perchance he may take warning or fear (God)." (2568)

"So far Pharaoh, in his inordinate vanity, had forgotten himself and forgotten how small a creature he was before

God. This was to be brought to his recollection, so that he might perhaps repent and believe, or at least be deterred by fear from "transgressing all bounds". Some men eschew wrong from sincere love of God and understanding of their fellow men, and some (of coarser minds) from the fear of consequences. Even the latter conduct may be a step to the former." FN2568

(20:45): "They (Moses and Aaron) said: "Our Lord! We fear lest he hasten with insolence (2569) against us, or lest he transgress all bounds."

"They were now in Egypt (see n. 2565 above) and therefore in the power of the Pharaoh. The local atmosphere called for the greatest courage and firmness on their part to carry out the dangerous mission which had been entrusted to them." FN2569

(20:46): "He said: 'Fear not: for I am with you: I hear and see (everything).'"

(20:47): "So go you both to him, and say, 'Verily we are messengers sent by your Lord: Send forth, therefore, the Children of Israel with us, and afflict them not:(2570) with a Sign, indeed, we have come from your Lord! and peace to all who follow guidance!" (2571)

"The Children of Israel were subjected to all sorts of oppression and indignities. They were given hard tasks; their leaders were unjustly beaten; they were forced to make bricks without straw; and they "groaned in bondage" (Exod.5:6-19, 6:5)." FN2570

"God, in His infinite Mercy, always offers Peace to the most hardened sinners, even those who are warring against Him. But, as stated in the next verse, their defiance cannot go on with impunity indefinitely. The punishment must inevitably come for sin, whether the sinner is great or small." FN2571

(20:48): "'Verily it has been revealed to us that the Penalty (awaits) those who reject and turn away.'"

The first encounter between Moses and Pharaoh

God instructed Moses and his brother Aaron to approach Pharaoh and warn him about the Day of Judgment, urging him to fear God and halt the persecution of the Israelites. However, God emphasised the importance of speaking to Pharaoh with gentleness and avoiding any form of shouting or threats, as this would provide Pharaoh with an excuse to dismiss God's Messengers as rude or aggressive.

I give below Verses 7:104-112, 20:49-59 and 28:36-39 with the relevant footnotes.

A) Chapter 7, Verses 104-112

(7:104): "Moses (1071) said: "O Pharaoh! (1072) I am a messenger from the Lord of the worlds,-"

"The story of Moses is told in many places in the Holy Qur'an, with a special lesson in each context. In 2:49 -71, the story is an appeal to the Jews from their own scripture and traditions, to show their true place in the religious history of mankind, and how they forfeited it. Here we have an instructive parallelism in that story to the story of Muhammad's mission — how both these men of God had to fight against (1) a foreign foe, arrogant, unjust, faithless, and superstitious, and (2) against the same class of internal foe among their own people. Both of them won through. In the case of Moses, the foreign foe was Pharaoh and his Egyptians, who boasted of their earlier and superior civilisation; in the case of the Prophet Muhammad the foreign foes were the Jews themselves and the Christians of his day. Moses led his people nearly to the Land of promise in spite of rebellions among his own people; Muhammad succeeded completely in overcoming the resistance of his own people by his own virtues and firmness of character, and by the guidance of God. What was a hope when these Makkan verses were revealed became an accomplishment before the end of his life and mission on earth." FN1071

"'Pharaoh' (Arabic. Fir'awn) is a dynastic title, not the name of any particular king in Egypt. It has been traced to the ancient Hieroglyphic words, Per-7ia, which mean 'Great House.' The nun is an "infirm" letter added in the process of Arabisation. Who was the Pharaoh in the story of Moses? If the Inscriptions had helped us, we could have

109

answered with some confidence, but unfortunately the Inscriptions fail us. It is probable that it was an early Pharaoh of the XVIIIth Dynasty, say Thothmes I, about 1540 B.C. See Appendix IV, on Egyptian Chronology and Israel, printed at the end of this Chapter." FN1072

(7:105): "One for whom it is right to say nothing but truth about God. Now I have come unto you (people), from (1073) your Lord, with a clear (Sign): 'So let the Children of Israel depart along with me.'"

"Notice that Moses, in addressing Pharaoh and the Egyptians, claims his mission to be not from his God, or his people's God but from 'your Lord,' from 'the Lord of the Worlds,' And his mission is not to his people only: 'I come unto you (Egyptian people) from your Lord.' The spirit of our version is entirely different from the spirit of the same story as told in the Old Testament, (Exod. chapters 1-15). In Exod. 3:18, the mission of Moses is expressed to be as from 'the Lord God of the Hebrews.'

The essence of the whole Islamic story is this: Joseph's sufferings and good fortune were not merely a story in a romance. Joseph was a prophet; his sufferings and his subsequent rise to power and position in Egypt were to be a lesson (a) to his wicked brothers who sold him into slavery, (b) to his people who were stricken with famine and found a welcome in Egypt, and (c) to the Egyptians, who were arrogant over their high material civilisation, but had yet to be taught the pure faith of Abraham. Israel prospered in Egypt and stayed there perhaps two to four centuries. (Renan allows only one century). Times changed, and the racial bigotry of the Egyptians showed its head again, and Israel was oppressed. Moses was raised

110

up with a threefold mission again (a) to learn all the learning of the Egyptians and preach God's Truth to them as one who had been brought up among themselves, (b) to unite and reclaim his own people, and (c) to rescue them and lead them to a new world, which was to open out their spiritual horizon and lead them to the Psalms of David and the glories of Solomon."FN1073

(7:106): "(Pharaoh) said: 'If indeed you have come with a Sign, show it forth, if you tell the truth.'"(1074)

"The ensuing dialogue shows the psychology on the two sides. Pharaoh is sitting in his court, with his ministers and chiefs around him. In their arrogance they are only amused at the effrontery and apparent revolt of the Israelite leaders, and they rely upon their own superior worldly power, aided by the magic which was a part of the Egyptian religion. Confronting them stand two men, Moses with his mission from God, and his brother Aaron who was his lieutenant. They are confident, not in their own powers, but in the mission they had received. The first thing they have to do is to act on the subjective mind of the Egyptians, and by methods which by God's miracle show that Egyptian magic was nothing before the true power of God." FN1074

(7:107): "Then (Moses) threw his rod, and behold! it was a serpent, plain (for all to see!" (1075)

"The serpent played a large part in Egyptian mythology. The great sun-god Ra won a great victory over the serpent Apophis, typifying the victory of light over darkness. Many of their gods and goddesses took the forms of snakes to impress their foes with terror. Moses's rod as a type of a *serpent at once appealed to the Egyptian mentality. The contempt which the Egyptians had entertained in their minds before was converted into terror. Here was someone who could control the reptile which their great god Ra himself had such difficulty in overcoming! (Cf.20:20)." FN1075*

(7:108): "And he drew out his hand, and behold! It was white to all beholders!" (1076)

"But the second Sign displayed by Moses was even more puzzling to the Egyptians, Moses drew out his hand from the folds of the garments on his breast, and it was white and shining as with divine light! This was to counter any suggestions of evil, which the serpent might have created. This was no work of evil - of black magic, or a trick or illusion. His hand was transfigured-with a light which no Egyptian sorcerers could produce. In Islam the "white hand" of Moses has passed into a proverb, for a symbol of divine glory dazzling to the beholders." FN1076

(7:109): "Said the Chiefs of the people of Pharaoh: "This is indeed a sorcerer well- versed."

(7:110): "His plan is to get you out of your land: then what do you advise?" (1077)

"The two Signs had the desired effect on the Egyptians. They were impressed, but they judged them by their own standards. They thought to themselves, 'These are ordinary sorcerers: let us search out our best sorcerers and show them that they have superior powers.' But like all worldly people, they began to fear for their own power and possessions. It was far from Moses's intention to drive out

the Egyptians from their own land. He merely wanted to end the Egyptian oppression. But the Egyptians had a guilty conscience, and they judged other people's motives by their own. They discussed the matter in council on quite wrong premises." FN1077

(7:111): "They said: 'Keep him and his brother in suspense (for a while); and send to the cities men to collect-'"

(7:112): "And bring up to you all (our) sorcerers well-versed."(1078)

1078" The advice of the Council to Pharaoh shows a misreading of the situation. They were in a panic about what the magic of this evidently powerful sorcerer could do against them. So they advised the Pharaoh to summon their most powerful sorcerers from all over the country, and in the meantime to hold Moses and Aaron in suspense — neither to yield to them nor definitely to oppose them. The Prophets of God could well afford to wait. Time is always in favour of Truth." FN1078

B) Chapter 20, Verses 49-59

(20:49): "(When this message was delivered), (Pharaoh) said: 'Who, then, O Moses, is the Lord (2572) of you two?'"

"Notice how subtly Pharaoh rejects the implication in Moses's speech, in which Moses had referred to 'your Lord' (verse 20:47). Pharaoh implicitly repudiates the suggestion that the God who had sent Moses and Aaron

could possibly be Pharaoh's Lord. He asks insolently, 'Who is this Lord of yours, of Whom you speak as having sent you?'" FN2572

(20:50): "He said: 'Our Lord is He Who gave to each (created) thing its form and nature, and further, gave (it) guidance.'" (2573)

"The answer of Moses is straightforward, dignified, and illuminating. He will not dispute about "my Lord" or "your Lord", the God of Israel, or the God of Egypt. He and his brother were proud to serve "our Lord," but He was the universal Lord and Cherisher, the One and Only God, Who had created all beings and all things. It was from Him that each created thing derived its form and nature, including such free will and power as man had got. He, Pharaoh, was subject to the same condition. In order that the free will should be rightly exercised, God had given guidance through His Messengers, and His Signs. Moses and Aaron stood as such Messengers, with such Signs. Will Pharaoh now understand and do right?" FN2573

(20:51): "(Pharaoh) said: 'What then is the condition of previous generations?'"(2574)

"But Pharaoh was not the man to accept teaching from the despised Israelite- one; two, who in his eyes was a renegade from the higher Egyptian civilization. If, he says in effect, 'there is only one God, to Whom all things are referred,' this is a new religion. What of the religion of our ancestors? Were they wrong in worshipping the Egyptian gods? And if they were wrong, are they in misery now? He wanted to trap Moses into scathing denunciations of his ancestors, which would at once have deprived him of the sympathy or the hearing of the Egyptian crowd." FN2574

(20:52): "He replied: 'The knowledge of that is with my Lord, (2575) duly recorded: my Lord never errs, nor forgets -'"

" Moses did not fall into the trap. He remembered the injunction given to him to speak mildly (20:44). He speaks mildly, but does not in any way whittle down the truth. He said in effect: 'God's knowledge is perfect, as if, with men, it were a record. For men may make mistakes or may not remember, but God never makes mistakes and never forgets. But God is not only All-Knowing: He is also All-Good. Look around you: the whole earth is spread out like a carpet. Men go to and fro in it freely. He sends abundance of water from the skies, which comes down in Nile floods and fertilises the whole soil of Egypt, and feeds men and animals (Cf. n. 1029 and n. 3646)." FN2575

(20:53): "He Who has, made for you the earth like a carpet spread out; has enabled you to go about therein by roads (2576) (and channels); and has sent down water from the sky. With it We have produced (2577) diverse pairs of plants (2578) each separate from the others."

"Sabil, in Arabic, means not only a road, but would include water-roads or channels, and in modern conditions airways-in fact all means of communication (Cf. 43:10)." FN2576

"This seems to be outside the speech of Moses, and connects itself with the following verses 54-56, as part of

the Word of God, expanding the speech of Moses and explaining the working of God's Providence in nature." FN2577

"Azwaj: we might translate, this Arabic word here, (as in 15:88) by 'classes' instead of 'pairs'; but as sex in plants seems to be referred to elsewhere" FN2578

(20:54): "Eat (for yourselves) and pasture your cattle: verily, in this are Signs for people endued with understanding."

(20:55): "From the (earth) We created you, and into it We shall return you, and from it We shall bring you out once again." (2579)

"This verse ought really to go into the last Section." FN2579

(20:56): "And We showed Pharaoh all Our Signs, but he did reject and refuse." (2580)

"This is a sort of general introduction to the confrontation between Moses and Pharaoh. The Signs are not only the countering of the fraudulent magic of Egypt with real miracles, but the subsequent Plagues (not mentioned here) and the Crossing of the Red Sea by Israel." FN2580

(20:57): "He said: "Have you come to drive us out of our land with your magic (2581) O Moses?"

"The Egyptians accused Moses of a design to deprive them of their land, and of exercising black magic. Both charges were palpably false. What Moses wanted to do

*was to free his people from bondage. The Egyptians had
all the power in their possession; they wished to use the
Israelites as untouchable helots: and anyone who wanted
to mitigate this injustice was branded as a dreadful person
who wished to deprive them of their lawful rights. As to
magic, the Egyptians judged Moses by themselves. They
practised sorcery to deceive the people. They accused the
Prophet of God of doing the same, though both his outlook
and source of his strength were altogether different."
FN2581*

**(20:58): "But we can surely produce magic to match
yours! So, make an appointment between us and you,
which we shall not fail to keep - neither we nor you - in
a place where both shall have even chances." (2582)**

*"Suwan: literally, 'equal, even.' It has been construed to
mean: (1) a place equally distant for both sides, a central
place, or (2) equally convenient to both sides, or (3) an
open level plain, where the people can collect with ease.
All these are possible meanings, but the one I have
adopted is more comprehensive, and includes the others,
viz.: (4) a place where both sides shall have even chances,
'a fair place', as Palmer laconically translates it." FN2582*

**(29:59): "Moses said: "Your appointed meeting shall
be on the Day of the Festival, (2583) and let the people
be assembled when the sun is well up."**

*" A great day of a Temple Festival, when the temples and
streets were decorated, and people were on holiday, free
from work (Cf. 26:38). Moses makes this appointment in
order to collect as large a number possible, for his first duty
is to preach the Truth. And he apparently did it with some*

effect with some Egyptians (20:70, 72-76), though the Pharaoh and his high and mighty officers rejected the Truth and afterwards Paid the Penalty." FN2583

C) Chapter 28, Verses 36-39

(28:36): "When Moses came to them with Our clear signs, they said: "This is nothing but sorcery (3367) faked up: never did we hear the like among our fathers of old!" (3368)

" This is what Moses was thinking of when he had said: 'They may accuse me of falsehood'. To accuse the purest Truth of lying is a favourite trick of those whose chief stock in trade is deception and sorcery and catching the attention of the vulgar by arts adapted to their ignorant minds!" FN3367

"'As to this higher talk of the worship of the One true God, why, our ancestors have worshipped power and patronage, as concentrated in Pharaoh, from the most ancient times!'FN3368

(28:37): "Moses said: 'My Lord knows best who it is that comes with guidance from Him and whose end will be best in the Hereafter: certain it is that the wrongdoers will not prosper.'" (3369)

"Cf. 6:135. The only argument in such a case is an appeal to God and to the ultimate Future. Both of these appeals require Faith. But even if you do not rely on anything so high, you can see that Falsehood or evils crystallised in

ancestral customs are not going to do anyone any good."
FN3369

(28:38): "Pharaoh said: 'O Chiefs! no god do I know for you (3370) but myself: therefore, O Haman! light me a (kiln to bake bricks) out of clay, and build me a lofty (3371) palace, that I may mount up to the god of Moses: but as far as I am concerned, I think (Moses) is a liar!'"

"Pharaoh claimed, himself, to be God-not only one god among many, but the only god: 'I am your Lord Most High': 79:24. At any rate he did not see why his people should worship anyone but him." FN3370

" I understand his speech to his minister Hainan to be sarcastic. But some Commentators have taken it very seriously and imagined that he actually thought of reaching the heavens by building lofty towers (Cf. 40:36)." FN3371

(28:39): "And he was arrogant and insolent in the land, beyond reason, - He and his hosts: they thought that they would not have to return to Us!" (3372)

3372 "They did not believe in the Hereafter. They did not understand that every deed must have its inevitable consequence, good, or evil, unless the Grace of God intervenes to save us from ourselves!" FN3372

Moses' encounter with the Egyptian magicians

I give below Verses 7:113-126 and Verses 20:60-76 in addition to the footnotes.

A) Chapter 7, Verses 113-126

(7:113): "So there came the sorcerers to Pharaoh: They said, 'of course we shall have a (suitable) reward if we win!'" (1079)

"The most noted sorcerers of Pharaoh came. Their art was built up on trickery and imposture, and the first thing they could think of was to make a selfish bargain for themselves. The Pharaoh and his Council would, in their present state of panic, agree to anything. And so they did. Pharaoh not only promised them any rewards they desired if they foiled the strange power of these men, but he also promised them the highest dignities round his own person. And so the contest begins, with due observance of the amenities observed by combatants before they come to close grips." FN1079

(7:114): "He said: 'Yes, (and more), - for you shall in that case be (raised to posts) nearest (to my person).'"

(7:115): "They said: 'O Moses! will you throw (first), or shall we have the (first) throw?'"

(7:116): "Said Moses: 'Throw you (first).' So when they threw, they bewitched the eyes of the people, and

struck terror into them: for they showed a great (feat of) magic." (1080)

" Moses and his brother Aaron were pitted against the most skillful magic-men of Egypt, but they were calm and confident and let the magic-men have their innings first. As is usual in this world, the magicians trickery made a great impression on the people, but when Moses threw his rod, the illusion was broken, and the falsehood was all shown up. In the Old Testament story (Exod. 7:10 -12) it was Aaron that threw the rod, and he threw it before the magicians. Aaron's rod became a serpent. Then the magicians threw their rods, and they became serpents, but Aaron's rod swallowed up their rods. The story given to us is more dramatic and less literal. We are told in general terms that Moses first allowed the magic-men to play their tricks. The rod of Moses was the symbol of his authority. It must have been a simple shepherd's crook with which he used to feed his flocks. With God's grace behind him, he was able to expose all false trickery and establish the Truth." FN1080

(7:117): "We put it into Moses's mind by inspiration: 'Throw (now) your rod': and behold! it swallows up straight away all the falsehoods which they fake!"

(7:118): "Thus truth was confirmed, and all that they did was made of no effect."

(7:119): "So the (great ones) were vanquished there and then, and were made to look small." (1081)

"The proud ones of the Court - Pharaoh and his chiefs - were hard-hearted, and the exposure of the imposture only

made them wreak their rage on those whom they could reach. On the other hand the effect on the humbler ones - those who had been made the dupes and instruments of the imposture - was quite different. Their conscience was awakened. They fell down to the ground in adoration of the Lord of the Worlds, and confessed their faith." FN1081

(7:120): "But the sorcerers fell down prostrate in adoration."

(7:121): "Saying: 'We believe in the Lord of the Worlds, -"

(7:122): "The Lord of Moses and Aaron."

(7:123): "Said Pharaoh: 'Did you believe in him before I give you permission? Surely this is a trick which you have planned in the city to drive out its people: but soon shall you know (The consequences).'" (1082)

" Pharaoh and his Court were doubly angry: first because they were made to look small when confronted by the power of God, and secondly, because their dupes and instruments were snatched away from them. These men, the sorcerers, at once recognised the Signs of God, and in their case the mission of Moses and Aaron was fulfilled. They turned back on their past life of imposture, make-believe, false worship, and oppression of the weak, and confessed the One true God. As usually happens, hardened sinners resent all the more the saving of any of their companions from sin and error. Judging other people's motives by their own, they accuse them of duplicity, and if they have the power, they take cruel revenge. Here the Pharaoh threatens the repentant

sinners with the extreme punishment for treason and apostasy (cutting off of hands and feet, combined with an ignominious death on the cross, as in the case of the worst malefactors). But they remained firm, and prayed to God for patience and constancy. Probably their influence spread quietly in the commonality. Ultimately it appeared on the Throne itself, in the person of Amenophis IV about five or six generations afterwards. See Appendix V, on Egyptian Religion, printed at the end of this Surah."
FN1082

(7:124): "Be sure I will cut off your hands and your feet on opposite sides, and I will cause you all to die on the cross."

(7:125): "They said, 'Indeed, to our Lord we will return.'"

(7:126): "'But you do wreak your vengeance on us simply because we believed in the Signs of our Lord when they reached us! Our Lord! pour out on us patience and constancy, and take our souls unto You as Muslims (who bow to Your Will)!'" (1083)

"These Egyptians, by their patience and constancy, show that their repentance was true. Thus in their case the mission of Moses was fulfilled directly, and their number must have amounted to a considerable figure. They were martyrs to their faith, and their martyrdom affected their nation in two ways. In the first place, as they were the pick of those who practised the false superstition in Egypt, their conversion and disappearance dealt a staggering blow to the whole system.

Secondly, the indirect effect of their martyrdom on the commonalty of Egypt must have been far greater than can be measured by numbers. The banner of God was planted, and the silent spiritual fight must have gone on ever since, though history, in recording outward events, is silent on the slow and gradual processes of transformation undergone by Egyptian religion. From a chaotic pantheon of animals and animal gods, the worship of the sun and the heavenly bodies, and the worship of the Pharaoh as the embodiment of power, they gradually came to realise the oneness and mercy of the true God. After many glimpses of Monotheism on Egyptian soil itself, the Gospel of Jesus reached them, and eventually Islam." FN1083

(7:127): "Said the chiefs of Pharao's people: 'Will you leave Moses and his people, to spread mischief in the land, and to abandon you and your gods?' He said: 'Their male children we will slay; (only) their females we will save alive; and we have over them (power) irresistible.'" (1084)

"Pharaoh's order against the sorcerers was drastic enough. But his Council is not satisfied. What about Moses and the Israelites? They had a seeming victory, and will now be more mischievous than ever. They appeal to Pharaoh's vanity and his superstition and sense of power. 'If you leave them alone,' they say, 'where will be your authority? You and your gods will be defied!' Pharaoh has a ready answer. He was really inwardly cowed by the apparent power of Moses. He dared not openly act against him. But he had already, before the birth of Moses, passed a cunning order to destroy the whole people of Israel. Through the instrumentality of midwives (Exod. 1:15), all the male children were to be destroyed, and the females

would then be for the Egyptians: the race of Israel would thus be at an end. This order was still in force, and would remain in force until the despised race was absorbed. But Egyptian cunning and wickedness had no power against God's Plan for those who had faith. See verse 129."
FN1084

B) Chapter 20, Verses 60-76

(20:60): "So Pharaoh withdrew: He concerted his plan, (2584) and then came (back)."

"Pharaoh was apparently taken aback at Moses appointing a solemn day of public Festival, when there would be a large concourse and there would sure to be some people not in the Court clique, who might be critical of Pharaoh's own sorcerers. But probably there was something more in their dark counsels, something unfair and wicked, to which Moses refers in his speech in the next verse." FN2584

(20:61): "Moses said to them: Woe to you! Do not forge a lie against God, lest He destroy you (at once) utterly by chastisement: the forger must suffer (2585) frustration!"

"Moses had some idea of their trickery and deceit. They would palm off their fraudulent magic as coming from God or from their gods! He warns them that their tricks will stand exposed, and their hopes will be defeated." FN2585

(20:62): "So they disputed, one with another, over their affair, but they kept their talk secret." (2586)

"They knew that they had here to deal with no ordinary man, but a man with powers above what they could conceive of. But evil always thinks evil. Judging Moses and Aaron by their own standards, they thought that these two were also tricksters, with some tricks superior to their own. All they had to do was to stand together, and they must win. I construe 20: 63-64 to be their private talk among themselves, followed by their open challenge to Moses in 20:65." FN2586

(20:63): "They said: 'These two are certainly (expert) magicians: their object is to drive you out from your land with their magic, and to do away with your most cherished institutions.'" (2587)

"Cf. 20:104. 'Your most cherished institutions,' i.e., 'your ancestral and time-honoured religion and magic'. Muthla, feminine of Amthal, most distinguished, honoured, cherished. Tariqah = way of life, institutions, conduct." FN2587

(20:64): "Therefore concert your plan, and then assemble in (serried) ranks: He wins (all along) today who gains the upper hand." (2588)

2588 "Presumably Pharaoh was in this secret conference, and he promises the most lavish rewards to the magicians if they overcome Moses. See 7:114. That-but I think more than that-is implied. That day was to be the crisis: if they won then, they would win all along, and Moses and his people would be crushed." FN2588

(20:65): "They said: 'O Moses! either you throw (first) or that we be the first to throw?'"

(20:66): "He said, 'you throw first'. Then behold their ropes and their rods-(2589) so it seemed to him on account of their magic - began to be in lively motion!"

"Their bag of tricks was so clever that it imposed upon all beholders. Their ropes and their rods were thrown, and seemed to move about like snakes. So realistic was the effect that even Moses felt the least bit of doubt in his own mind. He of course had no tricks, and he relied entirely on God." FN2589

(20:67): "So Moses conceived in his mind a (sort of) fear." (2590)

"The concerted attack of evil is sometimes so well-contrived from all points that falsehood appears and is acclaimed as the truth. The believer of truth is isolated, and a sort of moral dizziness creeps over his mind. But by God's grace Faith asserts itself, gives him confidence, and points out the specific truths which will dissipate and destroy the teeming brood of falsehood." FN2590

(20:68): "God said: 'Fear not! for you have indeed the upper hand:'"

(20:69): "Throw that which is in your right hand: Quickly it will swallow up that which they have faked. What they have faked is but a magician´s trick: and the magician thrives not, (no matter) where he goes."(2591)

"The meaning may be either (1) that falsehood and trickery may have their day, but they cannot win everywhere,

especially in the presence of Truth, or (2) that trickery and magic must come to an evil end." FN2591

(20:70): "So the magicians were thrown down to prostration: they said, 'We believe in the Lord of Aaron and Moses.'" (2592)

"Cf. this passage with 7:120-126 and 20:65-70 and the notes thereon." FN2592

(20:71): "(Pharaoh) said: 'You believed in Him before I give you permission? Surely this must be your leader, who has taught you magic! (2593) be sure I will cut off your hands and feet on opposite sides, and I will have you crucified on trunks of palm-trees: so you shall know for certain, which of us can give the more severe and the more lasting punishment!'"

"Pharaoh accuses his sorcerers who have been converted, of having been in league with Moses all the time, and in fact of having been led and taught by him! So arrogance and evil cannot conceive of God's worlds and worlds of beauty and truth beyond its own narrow vision! It is truly blind, and its very cleverness deludes is to wander far from the truth." FN2593

(20:72): "They said: 'Never shall we regard you as more than the Clear Signs (2594) that have come to us, or than Him Who created us! so decree whatever you desire to decree: for you can only decree (touching) the life of this world.'" (2595)

"Clear Signs: the miracles, the personality of the Messengers of God, the logic of events as they unfolded

themselves, and the light of inner conviction in their own conscience. There are, in addition, the Signs and Proofs of God in nature, which are referred to in many places, e.g., 20:53-54." FN2594

"Thus was the first part of the mission of Moses—that to the Egyptians— fulfilled. See n. 1083 to 7:126; also Appendix V." FN2595

(20:73): "For us, we have believed in our Lord: may He forgive us our faults, and the magic to which you did compel us:(2596) for God is Best and Most Abiding."

2596 "The magic, mummery, and deceptions which pertained to Egyptian Pagan religion became a creed, a State article of faith, to which all citizens were compelled to bow, and to which its priests were compelled actively to practise.

And Pharaoh was at the head of the whole system—the high priest or the supreme god. With justice, therefore, do the converted magicians lay the blame on Pharaoh, effectively negativing Pharaoh's disingenuous charge that they had been in league with Moses. These falsehoods and deceptions—combined in many cases with horrid cruelties, open and secret— were common to many Pagan systems. Some of them have been investigated in detail in Sir John G. Frazer's Golden Bough." FN2596

(20:74): "Verily he who comes (2597) to his Lord as a sinner (at Judgment),- for him is Hell: therein shall he neither die nor live."

"The verses 20:74-76 are best construed as comments on the story of the converted Egyptians who had 'purified themselves (from evil)'. But some construe them as a continuation of their speech." FN2597

(20:75): "But such as come to Him as Believers who have worked righteous deeds, - for them are ranks exalted,-"

(20:76): "Gardens of Eternity, beneath which flow rivers: they will dwell therein eternally: such is the reward of those who purify themselves (from evil)." (2598)

"As the Egyptian magicians had done when they confessed the One True God." FN2598

Chapter Four - The persecution of the Children of Israel by Pharaoh and his Chiefs

God tells us in Verses 43:51-56 about the speech delivered by Pharaoh to his foolish people, who blindly believed all the nonsense he uttered. He regarded Moses as a despicable contemptible wretch who could not explain himself eloquently. Pharaoh, in his arrogance and ignorance, claimed to be god and considered himself to be the best counsellor to his people.Sad to say, Pharaoh's attitude reminds me of many modern politicians who emulated his style and character and manipulated their followers.

Eventually, these rulers led their people to perdition in this life and to an eternal abode in the Hellfire in the Hereafter.

God mentions in Verse 40:46, the daily punishment of Pharaoh and his people and the eternal punishment in the next life: "It is the Fire before which they are presented morning and evening. And on the day when the Hour (of final judgment) will take place, (the order will be released,): "'Admit the people of Pharaoh into the most severe punishment'"

I give below Verses 43:51-56, which I mentioned above, regarding the most famous speech Pharaoh delivered to a House of Parliament packed with imbeciles who believed him, and how God dealt with them:

(43:51): "And Pharaoh called out among his people; he said, 'O my people, does not the kingdom of Egypt belong to me, and these rivers flowing beneath me (my palace); are you blind! Do you not see?'"

(43:52): "'Or am I [not] better than this one (Moses) who is insignificant and hardly makes himself clear?'"

(43:53): "'Then why are not gold bracelets bestowed on him, or (why) angels are not accompanying him in procession?'"

(43:54): "So he befooled his people, and they obeyed him. Indeed, they were [themselves] a people defiantly disobedient [of God]."

(43:55): "And when they angered Us, We took retribution from them and drowned them all."

(43:56): "And We made them a precedent and an example for the later peoples."

God is patient and He gives many, many opportunities to the most hardened sinners for repentance. But at length comes a time when His justice is provoked, and the inevitable punishment follows.Pharaoh and his hosts were blotted out and became a tale of the past. Their story is an instructive warning and example to future generations.

The following verses 2:49, 7:127, 7:141, 14:6, 28:4-8, 29:39, and 40:23-27 refer to the brutality of Pharaoh and his Chiefs towards the Children of Israel.

(2:49): "And [recall] when We saved you from the people of Pharaoh, who afflicted you with the worst torment, slaughtering your [newborn] sons and keeping your females alive (64). And in that was a tremendous trial from your Lord."

"The bondage of Egypt was indeed a tremendous trial. Even the Egyptians' wish to spare the lives of Israel 's females when the males were slaughtered, added to the bitterness of Israel. Their hatred was cruel, but their "love" was still more cruel. (Cf. 14:6). About the hard tasks, see in the Christian texts (Exod. 1:14): "'They made their lives bitter with hard bondage, in mortar and in brick, and in all manner of service in the field: all their service, wherein they made them serve, was with rigour.' Pharaoh's taskmasters gave no straw, yet ordered the Israelites to make bricks without straw: (Exod. 5:5-19). Pharaoh's decree was: 'Every son that is born ye shall cast into the river, and every daughter ye shall save alive': (Exod. 1:22.) It was in consequence of this decree that Moses was hidden three months after he was born, and when he could be hidden no longer, he was put into an ark of bulrushes and cast into the Nile, where he was found by Pharaoh's daughter and wife (28:9), and adopted into the family: (Exod. 2:2-10) (Cf. 20:37-40). Thus, Moses was brought up by the enemies of his people. He was chosen by God to deliver his people, and God's wisdom made the learning and experience and even cruelties of the Egyptian enemies themselves to contribute to the salvation of his people" (FN64).

(7:127): "And the eminent among the people of Pharaoh said, 'Will you leave Moses and his people to cause corruption in the land and abandon you and

your gods?' [Pharaoh] said, 'We will kill their sons and keep their women alive; and indeed, we are subjugators over them.'"

(7:141): "And [recall, O Children of Israel], when We saved you from the people of Pharaoh, [who were] afflicting you with the worst torment - killing your sons and keeping your women alive. And in that was a great trial from your Lord."

(14:6): "And [recall, O Children of Israel], when Moses said to his people, 'Remember the favour of God upon you when He saved you from the people of Pharaoh, who were afflicting you with the worst torment and were slaughtering your [newborn] sons and keeping your females alive. And in that was a great trial from your Lord.'"

(28:4): "Indeed, Pharaoh exalted himself in the land and made its people into factions, oppressing a sector among them, slaughtering their [newborn] sons and keeping their females alive. Indeed, he was an evildoer."

(28:5): "And We wanted to confer favour upon those who were oppressed in the land and make them leaders and make them inheritors."

(28:6): "And establish them in the land and show Pharaoh and [his minister] Haman and their soldiers through them that which they had feared."

(28:7): "And We inspired to the mother of Moses, 'Suckle him; but when you fear for him, cast him into

the river and do not fear and do not grieve. Indeed, We will return him to you and will make him [one] of the messengers.'"

(28:8): "And the family of Pharaoh picked him up [out of the river] so that he would become to them an enemy and a [cause of] grief. Indeed, Pharaoh and Haman and their soldiers were deliberate sinners."

(29:39): "And [We destroyed] Qarun and Pharaoh and Haman. And Moses had already come to them with clear evidences, and they were arrogant in the land, but they were not out-runners [of Our punishment]."

(40:23): "And We did certainly send Moses with Our signs and a clear authority."

(40:24): "To Pharaoh, Haman and Qarun; but they said, '[He is] a magician and a liar.'"

(40:25): "And when he brought them the truth from Us, they said, 'Kill the sons of those who have believed with him and keep their women alive.' But the plan of the disbelievers is not except in error."

(40:26): "And Pharaoh said, 'Let me kill Moses and let him call upon his Lord. Indeed, I fear that he will change your religion or that he will cause corruption in the land.'"

(40:27): "But Moses said, 'Indeed, I have sought refuge in my Lord and your Lord from every arrogant one who does not believe in the Day of Account.'"

Chapter Five - The Betrayal! Who turned against Moses?

We are told in Verses (28:76-83), the story of a man called Qarun from the people of Moses, who betrayed the trust and turned against his own people.Eighty miles to the southwest of the great Pyramids of Giza in Egypt, there is a salty lake called the "Lake of Qarun".According to the Qur'an, Qarun came from the people of Moses, but he openly opposed him, and his brother Aaron.He was wily, shrewd and wealthy and some speculated that he worked for the Pharaoh as a spy, reporting on everything that was happening among his own people.He was obsessed with the riches he was hoarding. The wealthier he became, the more miserly his conduct was. The keys of his treasure houses were so huge it took several strong men to carry them with difficulty, so you can imagine how much gold and silver he had amongst his treasures.

His own people warned him of the dangers of his obsession with wealth and power, but he didn't listen. "Exult not," they said "For God does not love those who exult in riches, but spend your wealth in God's cause. Nor should you forget your legitimate needs of this life. But do what is good as God has been good to you and do not seek occasions for mischief in the land."

Qarun believed it was entirely due to his own intelligence, skill and knowledge that he had gained his wealth. He was convinced that he was supreme to everyone else including Moses and Aaron. He contested their leadership at every opportunity saying "I am holier than you are. I have more wealth and status than any of you. I am far better qualified to be leader of the people."

On many occasions, he and his followers paraded through the streets of ancient Egypt showing how important he was in his fine clothes and jewels. Many people watching who were only concerned about their life in this world said, "If only we could have what Qarun has: He is very fortunate!"

Others who were wiser said "Sad for you. The reward from God is best for those who believe and work for what is right. Only those who act justly will receive this."

Qarun had followers who were willing to help him overthrow Moses and Aaron. But before they could take action, while Qarun went forth among his people in the pride of his worldly glitter, the earth split wide open. Qarun, his household, his treasures and all his men were swallowed into the depths. Nothing and no one could help them as they toppled over the edge of the chasm, desperately clutching at its sides in a vain attempt to stop themselves disappearing forever. A huge salty lake covered them all.

Not surprisingly, this act of Divine Intervention had an effect on those - who only the day before - wished they were as rich as Qarun. The Holy Qur'an records them as saying: "It is indeed God who provides or takes away as He pleases. Had it not been that God was gracious to us then we could also have been swallowed up! Those who rejected God will never prosper."

Men puffed up with wealth like Qarun are not pleasing to God, for wealth is for service not for hoarding or show.

137

History has known so many people like Qarun but where are they today?The Holy Quran teaches us that: It is the righteous that attain a prosperous end. If the rich think too exclusively of their wealth they become misers: they get their priorities all wrong and seem to forget their own spiritual needs. No wonder then that they also forget the needs of the poor and good causes which require support.Such people can cause more harm than good!

I give below the relevant verses for reference:

(28:76): "Qarun was of Moses' people but he oppressed them. We had given him so much treasure that (even) its keys would have weighed down a band of strong men. When his own folk said to him: 'Do not exult (in your riches), for Allah loves not the exultant,'"

(28:77): "'But seek (to attain) the abode of the Hereafter by means of that which God has given you, not neglecting your share of the world. And be benevolent just as Allah has been benevolent to you, and do not go seeking after corruption in the earth. Indeed, God does not love those who corrupt.'"

(28:78): "He said: 'I have been given this only on account of (certain) knowledge that I possess." Did he not know that God had destroyed earlier, in generations before him, those who were (materially) more powerful than him, and greater in number of followers? And the guilty will not be questioned about their sins.'"

(28:79): "And when he went forth among his people in all his finery, those who hankered after the life of this

world said: 'O that we had the like of that which has been given to Qarun! Surely he is endowed with great good fortune!'"

(28:80): "But those who had been given knowledge said: 'Alas for you! The reward of God is better for him who believes and does right, and only the patient shall receive this.'"

(28:81): "So We caused the earth to swallow him and his dwelling-place. He had then no host to help him against God, nor was he of those who could defend themselves."

(28:82): "And morning found those who had but yesterday coveted his lot, crying: 'No doubt of it! God indeed gives abundantly to whom He wills and sparingly to whom He wills. Had God not been gracious to us, He could have caused us to sink (in the earth likewise). Behold! The ungrateful will never prosper!'"

(28:83): "As for the abode of the Hereafter, We assign it to those who do not seek to exalt themselves in the earth, nor to spread corruption. The (happy) sequel is (only) for those who ward off evil."

We are also told in Verse 33:69, of another form of abuse which Moses had to deal with. And God in this Verse, is warning the believers not to do the same to Prophet Muhammad.

(33:69): "O you who believe! Be not like those who hurt Moses (by slandering him), but God proved him

innocent of that which they alleged; and indeed, he was well-esteemed in God's sight."

"The people of Moses often vexed him and rebelled against him and against God's Law. Here the reference seems to be to Num. 12:1-15. It is there said that Moses's own sister Miriam and his brother Aaron spoke against Moses because Moses had married an Ethiopian woman. God cleared Moses of the charge of having done anything wrong: 'My servant Moses is not so, who is faithful in all mine house.' Miriam was afflicted with leprosy for seven days as a punishment, after which she was forgiven, as also was Aaron. This is the Old Testament story.
The Prophet Muhammad was also attacked because of his marriage with Zaynab Bintjahsh but not by his own circle; his motives were of the highest and were completely vindicated as we have seen above." (FN3774)

Chapter Six - What does the Qur'an say about Passover (Pesach)?

Passover is often regarded as one of the most significant events in the history of the Children of Israel during their time in ancient Egypt. It is mentioned in many Verses in the Holy Qur'an.I often talk about it in my Friday sermons when I refer to how God deals with the oppressors.

In Verses (7:130-136), God tells us about the plagues He inflicted on Pharaoh and his people. He gave them many chances to repent and adjust their conduct, but they were arrogant and were a sinful people.

(7:130): "We punished the people of Pharaoh with years (of drought) and shortness of crops; that they might receive admonition."

(7:131): "But when good (times) came, they said 'This is due to us'; when gripped by calamity, they ascribed it to evil omens connected with Moses and those with him! Behold! in truth the omens of evil are theirs in God's sight, but most of them do not understand!"

(7:132): "They said (to Moses): "Whatever be the signs you bring, to work therewith the sorcery on us, we shall never believe in you.'"

(7:133): "So We sent (plagues) on them; wholesale Death, Locusts, Grain Weevils, Frogs, and Blood: signs openly Self-explained; but they were steeped in arrogance, a people given to sin."

(7:134): "Every time the penalty fell on them, they said: 'O Moses! On our behalf call on your Lord in virtue of his promise to you: if you will remove the penalty from us, we shall truly believe in you, and we shall send away the Children of Israel with you.'"

(7:135): "But every time We removed the penalty from them according to a fixed term which they had to fulfil— behold! They broke their word!"

(7:136): "So We exacted retribution from them: We drowned them in the sea, because they rejected Our signs, and failed to take warning from them."

So, before the punishment came to Pharaoh and his people, so many warnings were given to them. This is God's justice. God would always give respite to the sinners, so they might take heed, repent, believe and do righteous deeds.

I will now refer to Verses (10:75-93) to shed more light on the Passover.

(10:75) "Then We sent after them Moses and Aaron to Pharaoh and his establishment with Our signs, but they behaved arrogantly and were a criminal people."

(10:76): "So when there came to them the truth from Us, they said, 'Indeed, this is obvious magic.'"

(10:77): "Moses said, 'Do you say [thus] about the truth when it has come to you? Is this magic? But magicians will not succeed.'"

(10:78): "They said, 'Have you come to us to turn us away from that upon which we found our fathers and so that you two (Moses and Aron), may have grandeur in the land? And we are not believers in you.'"

(10:79): "And Pharaoh said, 'Bring to me every learned magician.'"

(10:80): "So when the magicians came, Moses said to them, 'Throw down whatever you will throw.'"

(10:81): "And when they had thrown, Moses said, 'What you have brought is [only] magic. Indeed, God will expose its worthlessness. Indeed, God does not amend the work of corrupters.'"

(10:82): "'And God will establish the truth by His words, even if the criminals dislike it.'"

(10:83): "But no one believed Moses, except [some] youths among his people, for fear of Pharaoh and his establishment that they would persecute them. And indeed, Pharaoh was haughty within the land, and indeed, he was of the transgressors."

(10:84): "And Moses said, 'O my people, if you have believed in God, then put your trust in Him if you submit (your will to His)'"

(10:85): "So they said, 'Upon God do we rely. Our Lord, make us not [objects of] trial for the wrongdoing people."

(10:86): "'And save us by Your mercy from the disbelieving people.'"

(10:87): "And We inspired to Moses and his brother, 'Provide dwellings for your people in Egypt, make your dwellings into places of worship, and establish regular prayers and give Glad Tidings to the believers.'"

(10:88): "And Moses said, 'Our Lord, indeed You have given Pharaoh and his establishment splendour and wealth in this worldly life, our Lord, that they may lead [men] astray from Your way. Our Lord, obliterate their wealth and harden their hearts so that they will not believe until they see the painful punishment.'"

(10:89): "[God] said, 'Your supplication has been answered. So remain on a right course and don't follow the way of those who do not know.'"

(10:90): "And We took the Children of Israel across the sea, and Pharaoh and his soldiers pursued them in tyranny and enmity. At length, when overwhelmed with the flood, he said: 'I believe that there is no god except Him Whom the Children of Israel believe in, and I am of those who submit (to God as a Muslim).'"

(10:91): "(It was said to him:) 'Ah Now!- But a little while before, you were in rebellion! And you did mischief (and violence)!"

(10:92): "'This day We will save you in the body, that you may be a Sign to those who come after you! And indeed, many among the people are heedless of Our Signs!'"

That was the inevitable fate of those who challenged God and disobeyed Him and spread mischief in the land. I find God's response to the statement made by Pharaoh while drowning and the preservation of his corpse to be amazing! Where is his body today? In the Egyptian Museum in Cairo, Egypt. These verses were revealed to Prophet Muhammad (pbuh), more than 1,450 years ago. A mummy that is purported to be Pharaoh's was discovered in 1898, less than 150 years ago. If today's oppressors and dictators reflected on this story, perhaps we could see greater peace in our world. But unfortunately, they are heedless as God stated above.

I will now refer to Verses 26:52 to 26:68 to show how God explained the events leading to Passover.(26:52): "By inspiration We told Moses: 'Travel by night with My servants; for surely you shall be pursued.'"

(26:53): "Then Pharaoh sent heralds to (all) the Cities"

(26:54): "(Saying): "'These (Israelites) are but a small band"

(26:55): "'And they are raging furiously against us;"

(26:56): "'But we are a multitude amply fore-warned.'"

(26:57): "So We expelled them (Pharaoh and his people), from gardens, springs"

(26:58): "Treasures, and every kind of honourable position;"

(26:59): "Thus it was, but We made the Children of Israel inheritors of such things."

(26:60): "So they pursued them at sunrise."

(26:61): "And when the two bodies saw each other, the people of Moses said: 'We are sure to be overtaken.'"

(26:62): "(Moses) said: 'By no means! my Lord is with me! Soon He will guide me!'"

(26:63): "Then We told Moses by inspiration: 'Strike the sea with your rod.' So it divided, and each separate part became like the huge, firm mass of a mountain."

(26:64): "And We made the other party approach thither."

(26:65): "We delivered Moses and all who were with him;"

(26:66): "But We drowned the others."

(26:67): "Verily in this is a Sign: but most of them do not believe."

(26:68): "And verily your Lord is He the Exalted in Might, Most Merciful."

In the story of Israel leaving Egypt, pursued by Pharaoh, we can see three contrasts:

1. The blind arrogance of the Egyptians, against the development of God's Plan.
2. The Faith of Moses, against the fears of his people.

3. The final deliverance of the Israelites against the destruction of the host of brute force.

The miracle was twofold:
   1. Moses and his people passed safely through the sea; and
   2. Pharaoh and his great host were drowned in the sea.

As it was then, so it is now. Despite the obvious Signs of God, people who are blind in their obstinance to Truth accomplish their own destruction, while humble, persecuted men of Faith are transformed by the Light of God and obtain salvation. Nothing that the powers of evil can do will ever defeat the merciful Purpose of God. Evil, in resisting good, will affect its own destruction.

Do Muslims celebrate Passover?

When Prophet Muhammad (pbuh), was in Medina, he noticed that the Jewish community were fasting. He asked them: "Why are you fasting?" They replied: "A great day!". "Why?" asked the Prophet. They answered: "It is the day when God saved Moses and the Israelites from Pharaoh and his army. Moses declared it as a fasting day for the Children of Israel to give thanks to God". The Prophet Muhammad (pbuh), said: "I have more to do with Moses than you."
Sahih al-Bukhari 2004, Book of Fasting, Hadith 31

And he declared it as a day of fasting for his followers. The day coincided with the 10th of the month of Muharram, the first month in the Islamic calendar. Muslims refer to this fast as the fast of "Ashura". Unfortunately, if you ask many Muslims today why they fast on this day, they have no idea.

On 22nd April 2024, I sent a greeting to my dear brother, the Rabbi at the local synagogue, wishing him and the Jewish community a blessed Passover. This is the response I received from him.

"Salaam my Brother Mohammed,

It is lovely to hear from you and I hope that you are enjoying your time in Spain.

We are in the final preparations for Pesach (Passover) and Rabbi D and I will each be with our families this evening, before being together for the morning service at Marlborough Road and our evening community Seder, which 120+ people are attending. During the table services this evening and tomorrow, we will be acknowledging with sadness the Israeli hostages and all the good and innocent lives lost, injured or displaced in Gaza and Israel.

We will continue to pray that the tyranny of the current Israeli government and, if I might say, the Hamas leadership will cease. Peace could come, if only people of good will would be leading both communities.

I hope we will be able to have coffee and break bread together after Passover has concluded and once you are back in South Woodford.

With every good wish"

Chapter Seven - The worship of the Golden Calf and God's forgiveness

The making of the golden calf and its worship by the Israelites during Moses' absence on the Mount are mentioned in the Qur'an in Verse 2:51, with further details provided in Verses 7:148-154 and Verses 20:83-98. Notice how in each case only those points are referred to which are necessary to the argument in hand. The storyteller whose object is to entertain his audience will narrate the full story from beginning to end. The teacher whose object is to deliver lessons will bring out the elements of the story necessary to paint a spiritual picture. Here, notice the contrast between the intense spiritual communion of Moses on the Mount and the simultaneous corruption of his people in his absence. We can understand his righteous indignation and bitter grief (7:150).

7:148. "The people of Moses made, in his absence, out of their (golden) ornaments, (1112) the image of a calf, (for worship): "(1113) it seemed to low: did they (1114) not see that it could neither speak to them, nor show them the way? They took it for worship and they did wrong."

"The people had melted all their gold ornaments, and made the image of a calf like the bull of Osiris in the city of Memphis in the wicked Egypt that they had turned their backs upon." (FN1112)

"Image of a Calf: The Arabic word "Jasad" is literally a body. In the present passage I understand many suggestions:

1. *that it was a mere image, without life;*
2. *as such, it could not low, therefore the appearance of lowing, mentioned immediately afterwards, was a fraud;*
3. *unlike its prototype, the bull of Osiris, it had not even the symbolism of Osiris behind it; the Osiris myth, in the living religion of Egypt, had at least some ethical principles behind it." (FN1113)*

"The lowing of the golden calf was obviously a deception practiced by the Egyptian promoters of the cult. Lytton in his "Last Days of Pompeii" exposes the deception practiced by the priests of Isis. Men hidden behind images imposed on the credulity of the commonalty." (FN1114)

(7:149): "When they repented, and saw that they had erred, they said: 'If our Lord have not mercy upon us and forgive us, we shall indeed be of those who perish.'"

(7:150): "When Moses came back to his people, angry and grieved, he said: 'Evil it is that you have done in my place in my absence: did you (1115) make haste to bring on the judgment of your Lord?' He threw down the Tablets, (1116) seized his brother by (the hair of) his head, and dragged him (1117) to him. Aaron said: 'Son of my mother! The people did indeed reckon me as naught, and went near to slaying me! Don't make the enemies rejoice over my misfortune, nor count me amongst the people of sin.'" (1118)

"Did you make haste . . . ? 'In your impatience, could you not wait for me? Your lapse into idolatry has only hastened God's wrath. If you had only waited. I was bringing to you in the Tablets the most excellent teaching in the commands of God.' There is subtle irony in the speech of Moses. There is also a play upon words: 'ijl= calf; and 'ajila = to make haste: no translation can bring out these niceties." (FN1115)

"In the verse 'Threw down the Tablets': we are not told that the Tablets were broken; in fact 7:154 (below) shows that they were whole. They contained God's Message. There is a touch of disrespect (if not blasphemy) in supposing that God's Messenger broke the Tablets in his incontinent rage, as is stated in the Old Testament: 'Moses's anger waxed hot, and he cast the tablets out of his hands, and brake them beneath the Mount.' (Exod. 32:10). On this point and also on the point that Aaron (in the Old Testament story) ordered the gold to be brought, made a molten calf, fashioned it with a graving tool, and built an altar before the calf, (Exod. 32:2-5), our version differs from that of the Old Testament. We cannot believe that Aaron, who was appointed by God to assist Moses as God's Messenger, could descend so low as to seduce the people into idolatry, whatever his human weaknesses might be." (FN1116)

"Moses was but human. Remembering the charge he had given to Aaron (7:142) he had a just grievance at the turn events had taken. But he did not wreak his vengeance on the Tablets of God's Law by breaking them. He laid hands on his brother, and his brother at once explained, (Cf. 20:94)." (FN1117)

"Aaron's speech is full of tenderness and regret. He addresses Moses as 'son of my mother'- an affectionate term. He explains how the turbulent people nearly killed him for resisting them. And he states in the clearest terms that the idolatry neither originated with him nor had his consent. In 20:85 we are told that a fellow described as the Samiri had led them astray. We shall discuss this when we come to that passage." (FN1118)

(7:151): "Moses prayed: 'O my Lord! forgive me and my brother! (1119) admit us to Your mercy! for You are the Most Merciful of those who show mercy!'"

"As Moses was convinced that his brother was guiltless, his wrath was turned to gentleness. He prayed for forgiveness-for himself and his brother: for himself because of his wrath and for his brother because he had been unable to suppress idolatry among his people. And like a true leader that he is, he identifies himself with his lieutenant for all that has happened. Even more, he identifies himself with his whole people in his prayer in verse 155 below. Herein, again, is a type of what the Holy Prophet Muhammad did for his people." (FN1119)

(7:152): "Those who took the calf (for worship) will indeed be overwhelmed with wrath from their Lord, and with shame in this life:(1120) thus do We recompense those who invent (falsehoods)."

"The consequences were twofold: (1) spiritual, in that God's grace is withdrawn, and (2) even in the present life of this world, in that godly men also shun the sinner's company, and he is isolated" (FN1120)

(7:153): "But those who do wrong but repent thereafter and (truly) believe, - verily your Lord is thereafter Oft-Forgiving, Most Merciful."

(7:154): "When the anger of Moses was appeased, he took up the tablets: in the writing thereon was guidance and Mercy for such as fear their Lord."

Now, I turn your attention towards the Verses below (20:83-98), which shed more light regarding the worship of the golden calf.

In these Verses, we are told how Moses was directed to lead his people and quell their rebellious spirit, and how that spirit was stirred up by Samiri. Samiri was the mischief-monger who convinced the Israelites to turn their golden ornaments into a calf to worship, instead of worshiping the One True God who saved them from Pharaoh and his hosts. Samiri was severely punished by God in this life and a greater punishment is awaiting him in the Hereafter.

(20:83): "(When Moses was up on the Mount, (2604) God said:) 'What made you hasten in advance of your people, O Moses?'"

"This was when Moses was up on the Mount for forty days and forty nights: 2:51 and n. 66. Moses had left the elders of Israel with Aaron behind him: Exod. 24:14. While he was in a state of ecstatic honour on the Mount, his people were enacting strange scenes down below. They were tested and tried, and they failed in the trial. They made a golden image of a calf for worship, as described below. See also (7:148-150) and notes." (FN2604)

(20:84): "He replied: 'Behold, they are close on my footsteps: I hastened to You, O my Lord, to please You.'"

(20:85): "" (God) said: 'We have tested your people in your absence: the Samiri has led them (2605) astray.'"

"Who was this Samiri? If it was his personal name, it was sufficiently near the meaning of the original root word to have the definite article attached to it: Cf. the name of the caliph Mu'tasim (Al-Mu'tasim). What was the root for "Samiri"? If we look to old Egyptian, we have Shemer = A stranger, foreigner (Sir E. A. Wallis Budge's Egyptian Hieroglyphic Dictionary. 1920, p. 815 b). As the Israelites had just left Egypt, they might quite well have among them an Egyptianised Hebrew bearing that nickname. That the name Shemer was subsequently not unknown among the Hebrews is clear from the Old Testament. In I Kings, 16:24 we read that Omri, king of Israel, the northern portion of the divided kingdom, who reigned about 903-896 B.C., built a new city, Samaria, on a hill which he bought from Shemer, the owner of the hill, for two talents of silver. See also Renan: History of Israel, 2:210. For a further discussion of the word, see n. 2608 below." (FN2605)

(20:86): "So Moses returned to his people in a state of indignation and sorrow. He said: 'O my people! Did not your Lord make a handsome (2606) promise to you? Did then the promise seem to you long (in coming)? Or did you desire that Wrath should descend from your Lord on you, and so you broke your promise to me?'"

"There are two promises referred to in this verse, the promise of God and the promise of the people of Israel. They form one Covenant, which was entered into through their leader Moses. See 20:80, and 2:63, n. 78. God's promise was to protect them and lead them to the Promised Land, and their promise was to obey God's Law and His commandments." (FN2606)

(20:87): "They said: 'We didn't break the promise to you, as far as lay in our power: but we were made to carry the weight of the ornaments (2607) of the (whole) people, and we threw them (into the fire), and that was what the Samiri suggested.'" (2608)

"In Cf. Exod. 12:35-36: the Israelites, before they left Egypt, borrowed from the Egyptians 'jewels of silver and jewels of gold, and raiment'; and 'they spoiled the Egyptians' i.e., stripped them of all their valuable jewellery. Note that the answer of the backsliders is disingenuous in various ways.

- *The Samiri was no doubt responsible for suggesting the making of the golden calf, but they could not on that account disclaim responsibility for themselves; the burden of the sin is on him who commits it, and he cannot pretend that he was powerless to avoid it.*
- *At most the weight of the gold they carried could not have been heavy even if one or two men carried it, but would have been negligible if distributed.*
- *Gold is valuable, and it is not likely that if they wanted to disburden themselves of it, they had any*

*need to light a furnace, melt it, and cast it into the
shape of a calf." (FN2607)*

*"If the Egyptian origin of the root is not accepted, we have
a Hebrew origin in "Shomer" a guard, watchman, sentinel;
allied to the Arabic Samara, yasmuru, to keep awake by
night, to converse by night: samir, one who keeps awake
by night. The Samiri may have been a watchman, in fact or
by nickname." (FN2608)*

**(20:88): "Then he brought out (of the fire) before the
(people) the image of a calf:(2609) It seemed to
low:(2610) so they said: 'This is your god, and the god
of Moses, but (Moses) has forgotten!'" (2611)**

*"See n. 1113 to 7:148, where the same words are used
and explained." (FN2609)*

" See n. 1114 to 7:148." (FN2610)

*"Regarding Moses has forgotten: i.e., 'forgotten both us
and his god. He has been gone for so many days. He is
searching for a god on the Mount when his god is really
here!' This is spoken by the Samiri and his partisans, but
the people as a whole accepted it, and it therefore
becomes their speech." (FN2611)*

**(20:89): "Could they not see that it could not return
them a word (for answer), and that it had no power
either to harm them or to do them good?" (2612)**

*"This is a parenthetical comment. How blind the people
were! They had seen Signs of the True Living God, and yet
they were willing to worship a dead image! The True Living*

God had spoken in definite words of command, while this calf could only emit some sounds of lowing, which were themselves contrived by the fraud of the priests. This image could do neither good nor harm, while God was the Cherisher and Sustainer of the Universe, Whose Mercy was unbounded and Whose Wrath was terrible" (FN2612)

(20:90): "Aaron had already, before this said to them: 'O my people! You are being tested in this: (2613) for verily your Lord is (God) Most Gracious; so follow me and obey my command.'" (2614)

"Resist this temptation: you are being tested in this. Do not follow after the semi-Egyptian Samiri, but obey me." (FN2613)

"The Bible story makes Aaron the culprit, which is inconsistent with his office as the high priest of God and the right hand of Moses. See n. 1116 to 7:150. Our version is more consistent, and explains, through the example of the Samiri, the lingering influences of the Egyptian cult of Osiris the bull-god." (FN2614)

(20:91): "They had said:(2615) 'We will not abandon this cult, but we will devote ourselves to it until Moses returns to us.'" (2616)

"Obviously Aaron's speech in the last verse, and the rebels' defiance in this verse, were spoken before the return of Moses from the Mount." (FN2615).

"The rebels had so little faith that they had given Moses up for lost, and never expected to see him again." (FN2616)

(20:92): "(Moses) said: 'O Aaron! what kept you back, when you saw them going wrong,'"

(20:93): "'From following me? Did you then disobey my order?'" (2617)

"Moses, when he came back, was full of anger and grief. His speech to Aaron is one of rebuke, and he was also inclined to handle him roughly: see next verse. The order he refers to is that stated in 7:142. 'Act for me amongst my people: do right, and follow not the way of those who do mischief.'" (FN2617)

(20:94): "(Aaron) replied: 'O son of my mother! Seize (me) not by my beard nor by (the hair of) my head! (2618) Truly I feared lest you should say; You have caused a division among the children of Israel, and you did not respect my word!'" (2619)

"Cf. 7:150" (FN2618).

"This reply of Aaron's is in no way inconsistent with the reply as noted in 7:150. On the contrary, there is a dramatic aptness in the different points emphasised on each occasion. In S. 7 we were discussing the Ummah of Israel, and Aaron rightly says: 'The people did indeed reckon me as naught, and went near to slay me!' In addition, 'Let not the enemies rejoice over my misfortune' he is referring by implication to his brother's wish to maintain unity among the people. Here the unity is the chief point to emphasise: we are dealing with the Samiri as mischief-monger, and he could best be dealt with by Moses, who proceeds to do so." (FN2619).

(20:95): "(Moses) said: 'What then is your case, O Samiri?'" (2620)

"Moses now turns to the Samiri, and the Samiri's reply in the next verse sums up his character in a few wonderful strokes of character-painting. The lesson of the whole of this episode is the fall of a human soul that nominally comes to God's Truth in a humble position but makes mischief when and as it finds occasion. It is no less dangerous and culpable than the arrogant soul, typified by pharaoh, which gets into high places and makes its leadership the cause of ruin of a whole nation. (FN2620)

(20:96): "He replied: 'I saw what they didn't see: so I took a handful (of dust) from the footprint of the Messenger, and threw it (into the calf): thus did my soul suggest to me.'" (2621)

"This answer of the Samiri is a fine example of unblushing effrontery, careful evasion of issues, and invented falsehoods. He takes upon himself to pretend that he had far more insight than anybody else: he saw what the vulgar crowd did not see. He saw something supernatural. 'The Messenger' is construed by many Commentators to mean the angel Gabriel. Rasul (plural, rusul) is used in several places for 'angels' e.g., in 11:69, 77; 19:19; and 35:1. But if we take it to mean the Messenger Moses, it means that the Samiri saw something sacred or supernatural in his footprints: perhaps he thinks a little flattery would make Moses forgive him. The dust became sacred, and his throwing it into the calf made the calf utter a lowing sound! As if that was the point at issue! He does not answer the charge of making an image for worship. But finally, with

arrogant effrontery, he says, 'Well, that is what my soul suggested to me, and that should be enough!' (FN2621)

(20:97): "(Moses) said: 'Then go! but your (punishment) in this life will be that you will say,(2622)´touch me not´; and moreover (for a future penalty) you have a promise that will not fail:(2623) Now look at your god, of whom you have become a devoted worshipper: We will certainly (melt) it in a blazing fire and scatter it broadcast in the sea!'" (2624)

"He and his kind were to become social lepers, untouchables; perhaps also sufficiently arrogant to hold others at arm's length, and say 'Noli me tangere' (touch me not)." (FN2622)

"Namely, the promised Wrath of God: see 20:81; 89:25" (FN2623).

"The cast effigy was re-melted and destroyed. Thus ends the Samiri's story, of which the lessons are indicated in n. 2620 above. It may be interesting to pursue the transformations of the word Samiri in later times. For its origin see notes 2605 and 2608 above. Whether the root of Samiri was originally Egyptian or Hebrew does not affect the later history. Four facts may be noted:
- *There was a man bearing a name of that kind at the time of Moses, and he led a revolt against Moses and was cursed by Moses.*
- *In the time of King Omri (903-896 B.C.) of the northern kingdom of Israel, there was a man called Shemer, from whom, according to the Bible, was bought a hill on which was built the new capital of the kingdom, the town of Samaria.*

- The name of the hill was Shomer (= watchman, vigilant guardian), and that form of the name also appears as the name of a man (see 2 Kings 22:21); some authorities think the town was called after the hill and not after the man (Hastings's Encyclopaedia of Religions and Ethics}, but this is, for our present purposes, immaterial.
- There was and is a dissenting community of Israelites called Samaritans, who have their own separate Pentateuch and Targum, who claim to be the true Children of Israel, and who hold the Orthodox Jews in contempt as the latter hold them in contempt: they claim to be the true guardians (Shomerim) of the Law, and that is probably the true origin of the name Samaritan, which may go further back in time than the foundation of the town of Samaria. I think it is probable that the schism originated from the time of Moses, and that the curse of Moses on the Samiri explains the position." (FN2624)

(20:98): "'But the god of you all is the One God. There is no god but He: all things He comprehends in His knowledge.'"

"You Shall Not Murder!" - The Story of a Killer and a Yellow Cow to Sacrifice:

God tells us in Verses 2:67-73 in the Qur'an, the story of a young man, at the time of Prophet Moses, who violated one of the Ten Commandments in the Torah and killed his uncle. The murderer wanted to speed up his uncle's death to inherit from him. He placed the corpse in a field to divert attention from himself.

When the people found the body of the deceased man, they immediately informed Moses. He told them that God is commanding them to slaughter a cow. The people accused Moses of making fun of them, but they didn't want to kill a cow because their hearts were still fully saturated with the golden calf they worshipped, as mentioned by God in Verse

(2:93): "And [recall] when We took your covenant and raised over you the mount, [saying], 'Take what We have given you with determination and listen.' They said [instead], 'We hear and disobey.' And their hearts absorbed [the worship of] the calf because of their disbelief. Say, 'How wretched is that which your faith enjoins upon you, if you should be believers."

So, they kept asking Moses many questions about the cow to delay the slaughter.

God told Moses to inform them that the colour of the cow is bright yellow like gold. This was meant to remind them of the golden calf which was still in their hearts. So, by killing the yellow cow they would purify their hearts from this false worship. When they found the yellow cow and killed it, God commanded Moses to take a piece of the cow's flesh and strike the body of the dead man with it. Immediately, he came back to life and pointed at his killer who was executed by Moses in accordance with the Law.

I give below the relevant Verses in the Qur'an and the footnotes, which refer to the story given above.

(2:67): "And [recall] when Moses said to his people, 'Indeed, God commands you to slaughter a cow (80).' They said, 'Do you take us in ridicule?' He said, "I seek refuge in God from being among the ignorant."

"This story or parable of the heifer in 2:67-71 should be read with the parable of the dead man brought to life in 2:72-73. The stories were accepted in Jewish traditions, which are themselves based on certain sacrificial directions in the Old Testament. The heifer story of Jewish tradition is based on Num. 19:1-10, in which Moses and Aaron ordered the Israelites to sacrifice a red heifer without spot or blemish; her body was to be burnt and the ashes were to be kept for the purification of the congregation from sin. The parable of the dead man we shall refer to later.

The lesson of the heifer parable is plain, Moses announced the sacrifice to the Israelites, and they treated it as a jest. When Moses continued solemnly to ask for the sacrifice, they put him off on one pretext and another, asking a number of questions which they could have answered themselves if they had listened to Moses's directions. Their questions were carping criticisms rather than the result of a desire for information. It was a mere thin pretence that they were genuinely seeking guidance.

When at last they were driven into a corner, they made the sacrifice, but the will was wanting, which would have made the sacrifice efficacious for purification from sin. The real reason for their prevarications was their guilty conscience, as we see in the parable of the dead man (2:72-73)." FN80

(2:68): "They said, 'Call upon your Lord to make clear to us what it is.' [Moses] said, '[God] says, 'It is a cow which is neither old nor virgin, but median between that,' so do what you are commanded.'"

(2.69): "They said, 'Call upon your Lord to show us what is her colour.' He said, 'He says, 'It is a yellow cow, bright in colour - pleasing to the observers.'"

(2:70): "They said, 'Call upon your Lord to make clear to us what it is. Indeed, [all] cows look alike to us. And indeed we, if God wills, will be guided.'"

(2:71): "He said, 'He says: It is a cow neither trained to plow the earth nor to irrigate the field, one free from fault with no spot upon her.' They said, 'Now you have come with the truth.' So they slaughtered her, but they could hardly do it."

(2:72): "And [recall] when you slew a man (81) and disputed over it, but God was to bring out that which you were concealing."

"In Deut. 21:1-9 it is ordained that if the body of a slain man be found in a field and the slayer is not known, a heifer shall be beheaded, and the elders of the city next to the slain man's domicile shall wash their hands over the *heifer and say that they neither did the deed nor saw it done, thus clearing themselves from the blood-guilt.*

The Jewish story based on this was that in a certain case of this kind, everyone tried to clear himself of guilt and lay the blame at the door of others. In the first place they tried to prevaricate and prevent a heifer being slain as in the last parable. When she was slain, God by a miracle, disposed of the real person. A portion of the sacrificed heifer was ordered to be placed on the corpse, which came to life and disclosed the whole story of the crime.

The lesson of this parable is that men may try to hide their crime individually or collectively, but God will bring them to light in unexpected ways. Applying this further to Jewish national history, the argument is developed in the following verses that the Children of Israel played fast and loose with their own rites and traditions, but they could not thus evade the consequences of their own sin." FN81(2:73): "So, We said, 'Strike the slain man with part of it.' Thus does God bring the dead to life, and He shows you His signs that you might reason."

Chapter Eight - God's wrath on those who disobeyed Moses and refused to enter the Holy Land

In Verses 5:20-26, God tells us about those who incurred His wrath when they refused to enter the Holy Land. He caused them to wander in the wilderness of Sinai desert for 40 years.

(5:20): "Remember Moses said to his people: 'O my people! Call in remembrance the favour of God unto you, when He produced prophets among you, (721) made you kings, (722) and gave you what He had not given to any other among the peoples.'" (723)

"There was a long line of patriarchs and prophets before Moses, e.g. Isaac, Jacob, Joseph etc." (FN721)

"From the slavery of Egypt, the Children of Israel were made free and independent, and thus each man became as it were a king, if only he had obeyed God and followed the lead of Moses." (FN722)

"Cf. Exod. 19:5: 'Now, therefore, if ye will obey my voice indeed, and keep my covenant, then ye shall be a peculiar treasure unto me above all people.' Israel was chosen to be the vehicle of God's message, the highest honour which any nation can receive." (FN723)

(5:21): "'O my people! Enter (724) the holy land which God has assigned unto you, and don't turn back

ignominiously, for then you will be overthrown, to your own ruin.'"

"We now come to the events detailed in the 13th and 14th chapters of the Book of Numbers in the Old Testament. Read these as a Commentary, and examine a good map of the Sinai Peninsula, showing its connections with Egypt on the west, Northwest Arabia on the east, and Palestine on the northeast. We may suppose that Israel crossed from Egypt into the Peninsula somewhere near the northern extremity of the Gulf of Suez. Moses organised and numbered the people, and instituted the Priesthood. They went south about 200 miles to Mount Sinai where the Law was received. Then, perhaps a hundred and fifty miles north, was the desert of Paran, close to the southern borders of Canaan. From the camp there, twelve men were sent to spy out the land, and they penetrated as far as Hebron, say about 150 miles north of their camp, about 20 miles south of the future Jerusalem. They saw a rich country, and brought from it pomegranates and figs and a bunch of grapes so heavy that it had to be carried by two men on a staff. They came back and reported that the land was rich, but the men there were too strong for them. The people of Israel had no courage and no faith, and Moses remonstrated with them." (FN724)

(5:22): "They said: 'O Moses! In this land are a people of exceeding strength: (725) Never we shall enter it until they leave it: if (once) they leave, then we shall enter.'"

"The people were not willing to follow the lead of Moses, and were not willing to fight for their 'inheritance.' In effect they said: 'Turn out the enemy first, and then we shall

enter into possession.' In God's Law we must work and strive for what we wish to enjoy." (FN725)

(5:23): "(But) among (their) God-fearing men were two on whom God had bestowed His grace: (726) They said: 'Assault them at the (proper) Gate: when once you are in, victory will be yours; But on God put your trust if you have faith.'"

"Among those who returned after spying out the land were two men who had faith and courage. They were Joshua and Caleb. Joshua afterwards succeeded Moses in the leadership after 40 years. These two men pleaded for an immediate entry through the proper Gate, which I understand to mean, "after taking all due precautions and making all due preparations". Cf. 2:189 and n. 203. But of course, they said, they must put their trust in God for victory." (FN726)

(5:24): "They said: 'O Moses! We shall never enter it as long as they are in it. Go you, and your Lord, and fight you two, while we sit here (727).'"

"The advice of Joshua and Caleb, and the proposals of Moses under divine instructions were unpalatable to the crowd, whose prejudices were further inflamed by the other ten men who had gone with Joshua and Caleb. They made an 'evil report,' and were frightened by the great stature of the Canaanites. The crowd was in open rebellion, was prepared to stone Moses, Aaron, Joshua, and Caleb, and return to Egypt. Their reply to Moses was full of irony, insolence, blasphemy, and cowardice. In effect they said: 'You talk of your God and all that: go with your God and fight there if you like: we shall sit here and watch.' (FN727)

(5:25): "He said: 'O my Lord! I have power only over myself and my brother: (728) so separate us from these rebellious people!'"

"'Moses and Aaron fell on their faces before all the assembly of the congregation.' (Num. (14:5). According to the words in the Old Testament story, God said: 'I will smite them with the pestilence, and disinherit them," (Num. 14:12). Moses prayed and interceded. But as we are told here, (a spiritual touch not found in the Jewish story), Moses was careful to separate himself and his brother from the rebellion." (FN728)

(5:26): "God said: 'Therefore the land will be out of their reach for forty years: (729) In distraction they will wander through the land: But don't sorrow over these rebellious people.'"

"The punishment of the rebellion of these stiff-necked people, rebellion that was repeated 'these ten times', (Num. 14:22) and more, was that they were left to wander distractedly hither and thither, through the wilderness for forty years. That generation was not to see the Holy Land. All those that were twenty years old and upwards were to die in the wilderness: 'Your carcasses shall fall in this wilderness.' (Num. 14:29). Only those who were then children would reach the promised land. And so it happened. From the desert of Paran they wandered south, north, and east for forty years. From the head of what is now the Gulf of 'Aqaba, they travelled north, keeping to the east side of the depression of which the Dead Sea and the river Jordan are portions. Forty years afterwards they crossed the Jordan opposite what is now Jericho, but by

that time Moses, Aaron, and the whole of the elder generation had died (Cf. 5:68). (FN729)

Chapter Nine - The persecution of the Children of Israel by the Babylonians and the Romans

This persecution is mentioned in Verses1-8 in Chapter 17, of the Qur'an. This Chapter is called Bani-Israel (the Children of Israel) as well as The Israa (a journey by night).But before mentioning the atrocities committed by the Babylonians and the Romans, let us consider Chapter 17, by itself. It opens with the night journey of the Holy Prophet Muhammad: he was transported from the Sacred Mosque (of Makkah) to the Farthest Mosque (of Jerusalem) in a night and shown some of the Signs of God.

The majority of Commentators take this Night Journey literally. The Prophetic Tradition literature gives details of this Journey and its study helps to elucidate its meaning. The holy Prophet was first taken to the site of the earlier revelations in Jerusalem and then ascended through the seven heavens, even reaching the Sublime Throne. This event is known as the Mi'raj in Arabic, which literally translates to "Ascension into the heavens."The Spaniard, Miguel Asin, Arabic Professor in the University of Madrid, has shown that this Mi'raj literature had a great influence on the Mediaeval literature of Europe, and especially on the great Italian poem, the Divine Comedy (or Drama) of Dante, which towers like a landmark in mediaeval European literature.

The reference to this great story of the Mi'raj is a fitting prelude to the journey of the human soul in its religious growth in life. The first steps in such growth must be through moral conduct-the reciprocal rights of parents and children, kindness to our fellow men, courage and firmness in the hour of danger, a sense of personal responsibility, and a sense of God's Presence through prayer and praise.

Here are verses 17:1-8 from the Qur'an, which refer to the persecution of the Israelites by the Babylonians and the Romans:

(17:1): "Glory to (God) Who did take His servant (Muhammad) for a Journey by night (2166) from the Sacred Mosque (2167) to the Farthest Mosque, (2168) whose precincts We did bless - in order that We might show him some of Our Signs: for He is the One Who hears and sees (all things)." (2169)

"The reference is to the Mi'raj for which see the Introduction to this Surah". (FN2166)

"Masjid is a place of prayer: here it refers to the Ka'bah at Makkah. It had not yet been cleared of its idols and rededicated exclusively to the One True God. It was symbolical of the new Message which was being given to mankind" (FN2167)

"The Farthest Mosque must refer to the site of the Temple of Solomon in Jerusalem on the hill of Moriah, at or near which stands the Dome of the Rock. This and the Mosque known as the Farthest Mosque (Al Masjid Al Aqsa) were completed by the Amir 'Abd al Malik in A.H. 68. Farthest, because it was the place of worship farthest west which was known to the Arabs in the time of the Prophet: it was a sacred place to both Jews and Christians, but the Christians then had the upper hand, as it was included in

172

the Byzantine (Roman) Empire, which maintained a Patriarch at Jerusalem. The chief dates in connection with the Temple are: it was finished by Solomon about B.C., 1004; destroyed by the Babylonians under Nebuchadnezzar about 586 B.C.; rebuilt under Ezra and Nehemiah about 515 B.C.; turned into a heathen idol-temple by one of Alexander's successors, Antiochus Epiphanes, 167 B.C.; restored by Herod, B.C. 17 to A.C. 29; and completely razed to the ground by the Emperor Titus in A.C. 70. These ups and downs are among the greater Signs in religious history" (FN2168)

"God's knowledge comprehends all things, without any curtain of Time or any separation of Space. He can therefore see and hear all things, and the Mi'raj; was a reflection of this knowledge." (FN2169)

(17:2): "We gave Moses the Book, (2170) and made it a Guide to the Children of Israel, (commanding): "'Take not other than Me (2171) as Disposer of (your) affairs.'"

"The Book: the revelation that was given to Moses. It was there clearly laid down that those who followed Moses must consider God as all-in-all. 'Thou shalt have no other gods before me; thou shalt not make unto thee any graven image . . . ; thou shalt not bow down thyself to them nor serve them: for I the Lord thy God am a jealous God . . . ;' etc. (Exod. 20:3-5).

These are the words of the English Bible. As a matter of fact, the spirit of Mosaic teaching went further. It referred all things to the Providence of God: God is the Disposer of all affairs, and we are to look to none but Him. This is Islam, and the Mi'raj showed that it was the teaching of

God from the most ancient times, and yet it was violated by the very people who claimed to be its custodians." (FN2170)

"Note the transition from 'We' in the first clause to 'Me' in the second clause. The first clause refers to the majesty of God as the Heavenly King: the second clause refers to His personal interest in all our affairs." (FN2171)

(17:3): "O you that are sprung from those whom We carried (in the Ark) with Noah! (2172) Verily he was a devotee most grateful."

"After the Deluge of the time of Noah the only descendants of Noah were those who were saved in the Ark with him. They had special reason to celebrate the praise of God. But they relapsed into idolatry, sin, and abomination. They are reminded of the true and sincere devotion of Noah himself, as contrasted with the unworthiness of Noah's descendants, especially the Children of Israel." (FN2172)

(17:4): "And We gave (Clear) Warning to the Children of Israel (2173) in the Book, that twice (2174) would they do mischief on the earth and be elated with mighty arrogance (and twice would they be punished)!"

"The Book is the revelation given to the Children of Israel. Here it seems to refer to the burning words of Prophets like Isaiah. For example, see Isaiah, chap. 24 or Isaiah 5:20-30, or Isaiah 3:16-26." (FN2173)

"What are the two occasions referred to? It may be that 'twice' is a figure of speech for 'more than once', 'often'. Or

174

it may be that the two occasions refer to (1) the destruction of the Temple by the Babylonian Nebuchadnezzar in 586 B.C., when the Jews were carried off into captivity, and (2) the destruction of Jerusalem by Titus in A.C. 70, after which the Temple was never rebuilt. See n. 2168 above. On both occasions it was a judgement of God for the sins of the Jews, their backslidings, and their arrogance." (FN2174)

(17:5): "When the first of the warnings came to pass, We sent against you Our servants given to terrible warfare: (FN2175). They entered the very inmost parts of your homes; and it was a warning (completely) fulfilled."

"A good description of the warlike Nebuchadnezzar and his Babylonians. They were servants of God in the sense that they were instruments through which the wrath of God was poured out on the Jews, for they penetrated through their lands, their Temple, and their homes, and carried away the Jews, men and women, into captivity. As regards 'the daughters of Zion, see the scathing condemnation in Isaiah, 3:16-26." (FN2175)

(17:6): "Then We granted you the Return as against them: (2176) We gave you increase in resources and sons, and made you the more numerous in man- power."

"The return of the Jews from the Captivity was about 520 B.C. They started life afresh. They rebuilt the Temple. They carried out various reforms and built up a new Judaism in connection with Ezra. See Appendix II following S. 5. For a time they prospered. Meanwhile their old

175

oppressors the Babylonians had been absorbed by Persia. Subsequently Persia was absorbed in Alexander's Empire. The whole of western Asia was Hellenized, and the new school of Jews was Hellenized also, and had a strong centre in Alexandria. But their footing in Palestine continued, and under the Asmonaean Dynasty (B.C. 167-63), they had a national revival, and the names of the Maccabees are remembered as those of heroes. Another dynasty, that of the Idumaeans, (B.C. 63 to B.C. 4), to which Herod belonged, also enjoyed some semi-independent power. The sceptre of Syria (including Palestine) passed to the Romans in B.C. 65, and Jewish feudatory Kings held power under them. But the Jews again showed a stiff-necked resistance to God's Messenger in the time of Jesus, and the inevitable doom followed in the complete and final destruction of the Temple under Titus in 70 A.C." (FN2176)*

(17:7) "If you did well, you did well for yourselves; if you did evil, (you did it) against yourselves. (2177) So when the second of the warnings came to pass, (We permitted your enemies) to disfigure your faces, (2178) and to enter your Temple (2179) as they had entered it before, and to visit with destruction all that fell into their power. (2180)"

"This is a parenthetical sentence. If anyone follows God's Law, the benefit goes to himself: he does not bestow a favour on anyone else. Similarly, evil brings its own recompense on the doer of evil." (FN2177)

"The second doom was due to the rejection of the Message of Jesus. 'To disfigure your faces' means to

destroy any credit or power you may have got: the face shows the personality of the man." (FN2178)

"Titus's destruction of Jerusalem in 70 A.C. was complete. He was a son of the Roman Emperor Vespasian, and at the date of the destruction of Jerusalem, had the title of Caesar as heir to the throne. He ruled as Roman Emperor from 79 to 81 A.C. (FN2179).

Merivale in his Ramans Under the Empire gives a graphic account of the siege and final destruction (ed. 1890, 7:221-255). The population of Jerusalem was then 200,000. According to the Latin historian Tacitus it was as much as 600,000. There was a famine and there were massacres. There was much fanaticism. The judgement of Merivale is: 'They' (the Jews) 'were judicially abandoned to their own passions and the punishment which naturally awaited them.' (7:221)." (FN2180)

(17:8): "It may be that your Lord may (yet) show Mercy (2181) unto you; but if you revert (to your sins), We shall revert (to Our punishments): "And we have made Hell a prison for those who reject Faith." (2182)

"Now we come to the time of our Holy Prophet Muhammad. In spite of all the past, the Jews could still have obtained God's forgiveness if they had not obstinately rejected the greatest of the Prophets also. If they were to continue in their sins, God's punishment would also continue to visit them." (FN2181)

"There is such a thing as disgrace in this life, but the final disgrace is in the Hereafter, and that will be irretrievable." (FN2182)

Chapter Ten - The persecution of the Children of Israel by the Philistines

David and Goliath

The story is narrated in Verses 2:246-251 of the Qur'an, which are given below, accompanied by footnotes that provide background context.

(2:246): "Have you not thought of the Children of Israel after (the time of) Moses (277)? They said to a prophet (278) (That was) among them: 'Appoint for us a king, that we may fight in the cause of God.' He said: 'Is it not possible (279), if you were commanded to fight, that you will not fight?' They said: 'How could we refuse to fight in the cause of God, seeing that we were turned out of our homes and our families?' But when they were commanded to fight, they turned back, except a small band among them. But God has full knowledge of those who do wrong."

"The next generation after Moses and Aaron was ruled by Joshua, who crossed the Jordan and settled the tribes in Palestine. His rule lasted for 25 years, after which there was a period of 320 years when the Israelites had a chequered history. They were not united among themselves, and suffered many reverses at the hands of the Midianites, Amalekites, and other tribes of Palestine. They frequently lapsed into idolatry and deserted the worship of the true God. From time to time a leader

appeared among them who assumed dictatorial powers. Acting under a sort of theocratic commission from God, he pointed out their backslidings, reunited them under His banner, and restored, from time to time and place to place, the power of Israel. These dictators are called Judges in the English translation of the Old Testament. The last of their line was Samuel, who marks the transition towards the line of Kings on the one hand and of the later Prophets on the other. He may be dated approximately about the 11th century B.C.." (FN277)

"This was Samuel. In his time Israel had suffered from much corruption within and many reverses without. The Philistines had made a great attack and defeated Israel with great slaughter. The Israelites, instead of relying on Faith and their own valour and cohesion, brought out their most sacred possession, the Ark of the Covenant, to help them in the fight. But the enemy captured it, carried it away, and retained it for seven months. The Israelites forgot that wickedness cannot screen itself behind a sacred relic. Nor can a sacred relic help the enemies of faith. The enemy found that the Ark brought nothing but misfortune for themselves and were glad to abandon it. It apparently remained twenty years in the village (Qaryah) of Ya'arim (Kirjath-Jearim): "I. Samuel, 7:2. Meanwhile the people pressed Samuel to appoint them a king. They thought that a king would cure all their ills, whereas what was wanting was a spirit of union and discipline and a readiness on their part to fight in the cause of God." (FN278)

"Samuel knew as a Prophet that the people were fickle and only wanted to cover their own want of union and true spirit by asking for a king. They replied with spirit in words, but

when it came to action, they failed. They hid themselves in caves and rocks, or ran away, and even those who remained 'followed him trembling': I. Samuel, 13:6-7." (FN279)

(2:247): "Their Prophet said to them: '(God) has appointed Talut (280) as king over you.' They said: 'How can he exercise authority over us when we are better fitted than he to exercise authority, and he is not even gifted, with wealth in abundance?' He said: '(God) has Chosen him above you, and has gifted him abundantly with knowledge and bodily prowess: God grants His authority to whom He pleases. God cares for all, and He knows all things.'"

"Talut the Arabic name for Saul, who was tall and handsome, but belonged to the tribe of Benjamin, the smallest tribe in Israel. His worldly belongings were slender, and it was when he went out to search for some asses which had been lost from his father's house that he met Samuel and was anointed king by him. The people's fickleness appeared immediately after he was named. They raised all sorts of petty objections to him. The chief consideration in their minds was selfishness: each one wanted to be leader and king himself, instead of desiring sincerely the good of the people as a whole, as a leader should do." (FN280)

(2:248): "And (further) their Prophet said to them: 'A Sign of his authority is that there shall come to you the Ark of the covenant (281), with (an assurance) therein of security (282) from your Lord, and the relics left by the family of Moses and the family of Aaron, carried by

180

angels (283). In this is a symbol for you if you indeed have faith.'"

"Ark of the Covenant: Tabut: a chest of acacia wood covered and lined with pure gold, about 5 ft. x 3ft x 3 ft. See Exod. 25:10-22. It was to contain the 'testimony of God', or the Ten Commandments engraved on stone, with relics of Moses and Aaron. Its Gold lid was to be the 'Mercy Seat.' This was a sacred possession to Israel. It was lost to the enemy in the early part of Samuel's ministry: see n. 278 to 2:246. When it came back, it remained in a village for twenty years, and was apparently taken to the capital when kingship was instituted. It thus became a symbol of unity and authority." (FN281)

"Security: sakinah = safety, tranquility, peace. Later Jewish writings use the same word for a symbol of God's Glory in the Tabernacle or tent in which the Ark was kept, or in the Temple when it was built by Solomon. (Cf. 9:26)." (FN282)

"Carried by angels: these words refer to the Tabut or Ark." (FN283)

(2:249): "When Talut set forth with the armies, he said (284): "'(God) will test you at the stream: if any drinks of its water, he doesn't go with my army: Only those who don't taste of it go with me: A mere sip out of the hand is excused.' But they drank of it, except a few. When they crossed the river, - he and the faithful ones with him, they said: 'This day (285) we cannot cope with Goliath and his forces.' But those who were convinced that they must meet God, said: 'How oft, by God's will, has a small force vanquished a big one? God is with those who steadfastly persevere.'"

"A Commander is hampered by a large force if it is not in perfect discipline and does not wholeheartedly believe in its Commander. He must get rid of all the doubtful ones, as did Gideon before Saul, and Henry V, in Shakespeare's story long afterwards. Saul used the same test as Gideon: he gave a certain order when crossing a stream: the greater part disobeyed and were sent back. Gideon's story will be found in (Judges, 7:2-7)," (FN284)

"Even in the small band that remained faithful, there were some who were appalled by the number of the enemy when they met him face to face and saw the size and strength of the enemy Commander, the giant Goliath (Jalut). But there was a very small band who were determined to face all odds because they had perfect confidence in God and in the cause for which they were fighting. They were for making a firm stand and seeking God's help. Of that number was David: see next note." (FN285)

(2:250): "When they advanced to meet Goliath and his forces, they prayed: 'Our Lord! Pour out constancy on us and make our steps firm: Help us against those that reject faith.'"

(2:251): "By God's will they routed them; and David (286) slew Goliath; and God gave him power and wisdom and taught him whatever (else) He willed (287). And did not God check one set of people by means of another, the earth would indeed be full of mischief: But God is full of bounty to all the worlds (288)."

"Note how the whole story is compressed into a few words as regards narration, but its spiritual lessons are dwelt upon from many points of view. The Old Testament is mainly interested in the narrative, which is full of detail, but says little about the universal truths of which every true story is a parable. The Qur'an assumes the story, but tells the parable.

"David was a raw youth, with no arms or armour. He was not known even in the Israelite camp, and the giant Goliath mocked him. Even David's own elder brother chided him for deserting his sheep, for he was a poor shepherd lad to outward appearance, but his faith had made him more than a match for the Philistine hosts. When Saul offered his own armour and arms to David, the young hero declined, as he had not tried them, while his shepherd's sling and staff were his well-tried implements. He picked up five smooth pebbles on the spot from the stream, and used his sling to such effect that he knocked down Goliath. He then used Goliath's own sword to slay him. There was consternation in the Philistine army: they broke and fled, and were pursued and cut to pieces.

"Apart from the main lesson that if we would preserve our national existence and our faith it is our duty to fight with courage and firmness, there are other lessons in David's story:

- *Numbers do not count, but faith, determination and the blessing of God;*
- *Size and strength are of no avail against truth, courage, and careful planning;*

- *The hero tries his own weapons, and those that are available to him at the time and place, even though people may laugh at him;*
- *If God is with us, the enemy's weapon may become an instrument of his own destruction;*
- *Personality conquers all dangers, and puts heart into our own wavering friends;*
- *Pure faith brings God's reward, which may take many forms: in David's case it was Power, Wisdom, and other gifts; see next note." (FN286)*

"David was not only a shepherd, a warrior, a king, a wise man, and a prophet, but was also endowed with the gifts of poetry and music." (FN287)

"God's plan is universal. He loves and protects all His creatures and His bounties are for all worlds (1:2 n. 20). To protect one, He may have to check another, but we must never lose faith that His love is for all in boundless measure." (FN288)

In my Friday sermon of 13th October 2023, I referred to the battle led by King Saul against Goliath and how David slew Goliath.

Chapter Eleven - The punishment of the Jewish fishermen who transgressed the Sabbath

Verses (7:163-166) tell the story of a Jewish fishing community in a seaside village, who transgressed in the matter of keeping the Sabbath. The fish surfaced for them only on the Sabbath and not on any other day.

The community was divided into three groups. One group, the Lawbreakers, was unable to resist the temptation to catch the fish on the Sabbath. Another group, presumably, the righteous ones, quietly disagreed with what the lawbreakers did. A third group, the righteous reformers, spoke out to the sinners and admonished them.

When the sinners disregarded the warnings that had been given to them, God rescued those who forbade evil; and He visited the wrong doers with a grievous punishment, because they were given to transgression.

(7:163): "Ask them concerning the town standing close by the sea. Behold! they transgressed in the matter of the Sabbath. (1137) For on the day of their Sabbath their fish did come to them, openly holding up their heads, but on the day, they had no Sabbath, they came not: thus did We make a trial of them, for they were given to transgression."

"Cf. 2:65 and n. 79. Fishing, like every other activity, was prohibited to Israel on the Sabbath day. As this practice was usually observed, the fish used to come up with a

sense of security to their water channels or pools openly on the Sabbath day, but not on other days when fishing was open. This was a great temptation to the law-breakers, which they could not resist. Some of their men of piety protested, but it had no effect. When their transgressions, which, we may suppose, extended to other commandments, passed beyond bounds, the punishment came." (FN1137)

(7:164): "When some of them said: 'Why do you preach to a people whom God will destroy or visit with a terrible punishment?' (1138) Said the preachers: 'To discharge our duty to your Lord, and perchance they may fear Him.'"

There are always people who wonder, no doubt sincerely, what good it is to preach to the wicked. The answer is given to them here:

1. *every man who sees evil must speak out against it; it is his duty and responsibility to God;*
2. *there is always a chance that the warning may have effect and save a precious soul. This passage has a special meaning for the times when Prophet Muhammad was preaching in Makkah, apparently without results. But it applies to all times." (FN1138)*

(7:165): "When they disregarded the warnings that had been given them, We rescued those who forbade Evil; but We visited the wrong-doers with a grievous punishment because they were given to transgression."

(7:166): "When in their insolence they transgressed (all) prohibitions, We said to them: "Be you apes, despised and rejected. (1139)"

"Cf. 2:65, n. 79." (FN1139)
"The punishment for breach of the Sabbath under the Mosaic Law was death. 'Everyone that defileth it (the Sabbath) shall surely be put to death: for whosoever doeth any work therein, that soul shall be cut off from among his people': (Exod. xxxi.14)." (FN79)

Chapter Twelve - The Jews did not Kill Jesus

Before God breathed into Mary's womb, and before she conceived Jesus, the Angels told her about his Message and his Miracles, as explained in Verses 3:42-51, in the Qur'an:

(3:42): "And [mention] when the angels said, 'O Mary, indeed God has chosen you and purified you and chosen you above the women of the worlds.'"

(3:43): "'O Mary, be devoutly obedient to your Lord and prostrate and bow with those who bow [in prayer].'"

(3:44): "That is from the news of the unseen which We reveal to you, [O Muhammad]. And you were not with them when they cast their pens as to which of them should be responsible for Mary. Nor were you with them when they disputed."

(3:45): "[And mention] when the angels said, 'O Mary, indeed God gives you good tidings of a word from Him, whose name will be the Messiah, Jesus, the son of Mary - distinguished in this world and the Hereafter and among those brought near [to God]."

(3:46): "'He will speak to the people in the cradle and in maturity and will be of the righteous.'"

(3:47): "She said, 'My Lord, how will I have a child when no man has touched me?' [The angel] said, 'Such is God; He creates what He wills. When He decrees a matter, He only says to it, 'Be,' and it is."

(3:48): "'And He will teach him the Book and wisdom and the Torah and the Gospel'"

(3:49): "'And [make him] a Messenger to the Children of Israel, [who will say], 'Indeed I have come to you with a sign from your Lord in that I design for you from clay [that which is] like the form of a bird, then I breathe into it and it becomes a bird by permission of God. And I cure the blind and the leper, and I give life to the dead - by permission of God. And I inform you of what you eat and what you store in your houses. Indeed, in that is a sign for you, if you are believers.'"

(3:50): "'And [I have come] confirming what was before me of the Torah and to make lawful for you some of what was forbidden to you. And I have come to you with a sign from your Lord, so fear God and obey me.'"

(3:51): "'Indeed, God is my Lord and your Lord, so worship Him. That is the straight path.'"

In Verses 3:52-53, God tells us about the resistance Jesus experienced from the Children of Israel:

(3:52): "But when Jesus felt [persistence in] disbelief from them, he said, 'Who are my supporters for [the cause of] God?' The disciples said, 'We are supporters for God. We have believed in God and testify that we are Muslims [submitting to Him].'"

(3:53): "'Our Lord, we have believed in what You revealed and have followed the Messenger (Jesus), so register us among the witnesses [to truth].'"

When the enemies of Jesus planned to harm him, God informed him of their evil plotting. He prepared him mentally for the miracle which he was going to witness, as stated in Verses 3:54-60

(3:54): "And the disbelievers planned, but God planned. And God is the best of planners."

(3:55): "[Mention] when God said, 'O Jesus, indeed I will put you to sleep and raise you to Myself and purify you from those who disbelieve and make those who follow you [in submission to God alone] superior to those who disbelieve until the Day of Resurrection. Then to Me is your return, and I will judge between you concerning that in which you used to differ.'"

(3:56): "'And as for those who disbelieved, I will punish them with a severe punishment in this world and the Hereafter, and they will have no helpers.'"

(3:57): "But as for those who believed and did righteous deeds, He will give them in full their rewards, and God does not like the wrongdoers."

(3:58): "This is what We recite to you, [O Muhammad], of [Our] verses and the precise [and wise] message."

(3:59): "Indeed, the example of Jesus to God is like that of Adam. He created Him from dust; then He said to him, 'Be,' and he was."

(3:60): "The truth is from your Lord, so do not be among the doubters."

God states in Verses (4:157-158) in the Qur'an that the Jews neither killed Jesus nor crucified him. It was made to look like that to them as someone else took his place on the cross. God saved Jesus and raised him, in body and soul, unto Himself.

(4:157): "And [for] their saying (in boast), 'Indeed, we have killed the Messiah, Jesus, the son of Mary, the messenger of God.' And they did not kill him, nor did they crucify him (663); but [another] was made to resemble him to them. And indeed, those who differ over it are in doubt about it. They have no knowledge of it except the following of assumption. And they did not kill him, for certain."

"The end of the life of Jesus on earth is as much involved in mystery as his birth, and indeed the greater part of his private life, except the three main years of his ministry. It is not profitable to discuss the many doubts and conjectures among the early Christian sects and among Muslim theologians. The Orthodox-Christian Churches make it a cardinal point of their doctrine that his life was taken on the Cross, that he died and was buried, that on the third day he rose in the body with his wounds intact, and walked about and conversed, and ate with his disciples, and was afterwards taken up bodily to heaven. This is necessary for the theological doctrine of blood sacrifice and vicarious

atonement for sins, which is rejected by Islam. But some of the early Christian sects did not believe that Christ was killed on the Cross. The Basilidans believed that someone else was substituted for him. The Docetae held that Christ never had a real physical or natural body, but only an apparent or phantom body, and that his Crucifixion was only apparent, not real. The Marcionite Gospel (about A.C. 138) denied that Jesus was born, and merely said that he appeared in human form. The Gospel of St. Barnabas supported the theory of substitution on the Cross. The Qur'anic teaching is that Christ was not crucified nor killed by the Jews, notwithstanding certain apparent circumstances which produced that illusion in the minds of some of his enemies; that disputatious, doubts, and conjectures on such matters are vain; and that he was taken up to God (see 4:158 and 3:55)." FN663

(4:158): "Rather, God raised him to Himself (664). And ever is God Exalted in Might and Wise."

"There is a difference of opinion as to the exact interpretation of this verse. The words are: The Jews did not kill Jesus, but God raised him up (rafa'ahu) to Himself. One school holds that Jesus did not die the usual human death, but still lives in the body in heaven, which is the generally accepted Muslim view. Another holds that he did die (5:117) but not when he was supposed to be crucified, and that his being "raised up" unto God means that instead of being disgraced as a malefactor, as the Jews intended, he was on the contrary honoured by God as His Messenger: (see 4:159). The same word rafa'a is used in association with honour in connection with Prophet Muhammad in 94:4." FN664

There is an authentic Prophetic tradition (Hadith) which sheds more light on the saving of Jesus and his ascension into heaven.It was a Friday mid-afternoon and Jesus was conversing with his disciples in his house. The house was surrounded by Roman soldiers, who were about to raid it, arrest him and crucify him.

Jesus said to his companions, "Who among you would volunteer to be made by God to look like me, and he will take my place on the cross, for which he will be my companion in Paradise?" A young man volunteered, but Jesus thought that he was too young. He asked the question a second and third time, each time the same young man volunteered, prompting Jesus to say, "Well then, you will be that man."

God made the young man look exactly like Jesus, while a hole opened in the roof of the house, and Jesus was made to sleep and ascended to heaven while asleep. Then the soldiers raided the house, arrested the man who was made by God to look like Jesus and crucified him and put thorns on his head to humiliate him.

This authentic Hadith is reported by Ibn Abi Hatim (4/1110) and An-Nasai in Al-Kubra (6/489).

In the year 2010, my wife and I were invited by the late Reverend R.H., from Trinity Church in South Woodford, London, to join him and a group from his church to travel to Germany to attend a passion play at the village of Oberammergau.

Before travelling, I had no idea what the play was about. The Germany Travel Guide stated "The life and death of

Jesus Christ has been depicted in a number of different mediums. One of the oldest forms of this is through a Passion Play. There is a famous Passion Play that is performed in Germany once every 10 years: the Oberammergau Passion Play. It is a worldwide spectacle that has been performed since 1634. Situated in the small yet significant village Oberammergau, Bavaria, this play has worldwide historical significance."

It continues: "A Passion Play or Easter Pageant is a dramatic presentation depicting the Passion of Jesus Christ: his trial, suffering and death. It is a traditional part of Lent in several Christian denominations, particularly in the Catholic tradition.

There are a number of passion plays which are performed all over the world, though a number of them were discontinued centuries ago. For example, the oldest Frankfurt Passion play was that of Canon Baldemar von Peterwell, which ran from 1350 to 1381.

The most famous and oldest passion play, which is still being performed to this day, is the Oberammergau Passion Play, first performed in the Bavarian village of Oberammergau in 1634 and now performed every 10 years.

The play is a staging of Jesus' passion, suffering, death and resurrection. The play covers the short final period of his life from his visit to Jerusalem and leading to his execution by crucifixion. It has been criticised as being antisemitic, but it is the earliest continuous survivor of the age of Christian drama."

The manner in which the play portrayed the Jews who planned and carried out the torture and the killing of Jesus, as blood thirsty, made me feel that it was antisemitic.Many Christians among the audience started to cry loudly. I was told that I was the only Muslim who had ever attended this play. I did not feel any emotion when I saw the suffering of Jesus on the stage, because as a Muslim, God told us that Jesus was neither killed nor crucified, but God saved him and raised him unto Himself. Imagine what would have happened if I had announced this to the Christian audience! They would have definitely crucified me on the stage next to Jesus.

When I came back to London, my friend Rabbi D.H. was so upset with me for having attended the play. I said to him: "You should have warned me before going!".

I am pleading with all my Christian brothers and sisters, to please stop the persecution of the Children of Israel as they are not the "killer of God", as some of you may claim.

I quote below from an article by Robert Crux | 2 November 2023 | Collateral Damage: A Primer on Evangelicals, Israel, and the War for the Holy Land – Adventist Today:

"Evangelicals assert that when the last days arrive, God will draw the Jewish people back to Israel, where they will rebuild the temple and eventually accept Jesus as the rightful Messiah. This historical and prophetic event will trigger the return of Jesus together with the rapture of true believers. For many evangelical Christians, the success of Israel is the 'touchstone of prophecy.'"

Muslims believe that Jesus remains alive in Heaven in the presence of his Lord until his return to earth as confirmed by God in the Qur'an, Verse

(4:159): "And there is none of the People of the Book but must believe in him (Jesus) before his death; and on the Day of Judgment he (Jesus) will be a witness against them."

Prophet Muhammad said, "The Hour of Judgment will not be established until the son of Mary [Jesus] descends among you as a just ruler. He will break the cross, kill the pigs, and abolish the jizyah tax. Money will be in abundance so that nobody will accept it (as charitable gifts)". (Al-Bukhari and Muslim)

In this hadith, Jesus (pbuh) breaking the cross refers to him refuting the invented story of his crucifixion and resurrection. And killing the pig means that he will prohibit the eating of its meat again, as it is in Islam and in the original Law of Moses.

And abolishing the jizyah (a tax paid by non-Muslims—instead of the zakah (obligatory charity paid by Muslims—in return for the equal rights, protection, and services they enjoy in a Muslim state), in this hadith, means that this ruling will be abolished, as all Christians will follow Jesus (pbuh) in his second coming and become Muslims. However, his coming will be preceded by the appearance of the Antichrist (the Dajjal, the Imposter), who will come to lead people away from the truth of Islam, by showing what appears to be miraculous actions—by the will of God—that will deceive only the naïve and unbelievers.

My dear Evangelical Christian brothers and sisters, no one can speed up Jesus' return as it is only decided by God. So please don't force the Jews to emigrate to Israel because of your belief that Jesus will only come back when certain Jews will settle there. Don't be selfish. You know very well that you are subjecting them to ongoing wars as the owners of the land will never give up their territories.

We must recall what Moses said to his people about who would inherit the land as stated by God in Verses (7:128-129):

(7:128): "And Moses said to his people, 'Seek help through God and be patient. Indeed, the earth belongs to God. He causes to inherit it whom He wills of His servants. And the [best] outcome is for the righteous.'"

(7:129): "They said, 'We have been oppressed before you came to us and after you have come to us.' He said, 'Perhaps your Lord will destroy your enemy and grant you succession in the land and see how you will do.'"

We must all remember that, if there is no justice, there will be no peace. Peace in Israel can only be secured if built on the hope, liberty, and dignity of the Palestinian people, according to Josep Borrell, the EU's foreign policy chief.

He said on Wednesday 22 November 2023:

"Peace will be built on the hope of the Palestinian people, their hope to live in liberty and dignity. Without this there will be no peace".

He added that Israel's security could only be achieved if the Palestinians had their own independent state.

I remember once I said to a very dear Jewish friend of mine, C.N., who was my lawyer for many years: *"Why can't the Jews and the Palestinians all live together in one country and have equal rights, like all of us living in the UK?"*

She replied: *"This means we will become a minority again!"*

Another Jewish friend of mine, J.K., who was a great academic, said: *"Although I'm neither a politician nor a Palestinian, I think a three-states solution would be more practical than a two- states solution because of the distance between the West Bank and Gaza. A three-states solution can be achieved by making Gaza an independent Palestinian state and making the West Bank as another state."*

May God help us all to make the right decision and may God's Peace prevail.

Chapter Thirteen - Who were those who were cursed by David and Jesus?

The Qur'an says in Verses 5:78-79:

(5:78): "Curses were pronounced on those among the Children of Israel who rejected Faith, by the tongue of David (786) and of Jesus the son of Mary (787): "because they disobeyed and persisted in Excesses (transgressed all limits)."

"The Psalms of David have several passages of imprecations against the wicked. Cf. Psalms 109:17-18; 78.21-22 ('Therefore the Lord heard this and was wroth: so a fire was kindled against Jacob, and anger also came up against Israel; because they believed not in God, and trusted not in His salvation'); Psalms 69:22- 28, and Psalms 5:10." (FN786)

"Cf. Matt. 23:33 ('Ye serpents, ye generation of vipers, how can ye escape the damnation of Hell?); also Matt. 12:34." (FN787)

(5:79): "Nor did they forbid one another (788) the iniquities which they committed: evil indeed were the deeds which they did."

"There are bad men in every community, but if leaders connive at the misdeeds of the commonalty, and even worse, if leaders themselves share in the misdeeds, as happened with the Pharisees and Scribes against whom

Jesus spoke out, then that community is doomed."
(FN788)

So, the lawbreakers among the Children of Israel are condemned by God in their own Books and by the tongue of their own Prophets like David and Jesus.

They are also condemned by God in the Qur'an as a warning to any lawbreakers among the Muslims.There are many Verses in the Qur'an where God condemns the hypocrites among the Muslims and promises them a great punishment in this life and in the Hereafter. For example, Verses 63:1-6:

(63:1): "When the hypocrites come to you, [O Muhammad], they say, 'We testify that you are the Messenger of God'. And God knows that you are His Messenger, and God testifies that the hypocrites are liars."

(63:2): "They have taken their oaths as a cover, so they averted [people] from the way of God. Indeed, it was evil that they were doing."

(63:3): "That is because they believed, and then they disbelieved; so their hearts were sealed over, and they do not understand."

(63:4): "And when you see them, their forms please you, and if they speak, you listen to their speech. [They are] as if they were pieces of wood propped up - they think that every shout is against them. They are the enemy, so beware of them. May God destroy them; how are they deluded?"

(63:5). "And when it is said to them, 'Come, the Messenger of God will ask forgiveness for you', they turn their heads aside and you see them evading while they are arrogant."

(63:6). "It is all the same for them whether you ask forgiveness for them or do not ask forgiveness for them; never will God forgive them. Indeed, God does not guide the defiantly disobedient people."

Also, those among the Muslims who wage war against God and His Messenger Muhammad (pbuh), are severely punished in this life (5:33-34) and a heavy punishment is theirs in the Hereafter, unless they repent, believe and adjust their conduct by doing good deeds.

(5:33): "The punishment of those who wage war against God and His Messenger, and strive with might and main for mischief through the land (738) is: execution, or crucifixion, or the cutting off of hands and feet from opposite sides,(739) or exile from the land: that is their disgrace in this world, and a heavy punishment is theirs in the Hereafter;"

"For the double crime of treason against the State, combined with treason against God, as shown by overt crimes, four alternative punishments are mentioned, any one of which is to be applied according to circumstances, viz. execution (cutting off the head), crucifixion, maiming, or exile. These were features of the Criminal Law then and for centuries afterwards, except that tortures such as 'hanging, drawing, and quartering' in English Law, and piercing of eyes and leaving the unfortunate victim

exposed to a tropical sun, which was practised in Arabia, and all such tortures were abolished. In any case sincere repentance before it was too late was recognised as a round for mercy." (FN738)

"Understood to mean the right hand and the left foot." (FN739)

(5:34): "Except for those who repent before they fall into your power: in that case, know that God is Oft-forgiving, Most Merciful."

Chapter Fourteen - The ongoing persecution of the Children of Israel who rejected faith

In the following Verses 7:167-170, God addresses the Children of Israel, warning them of His punishment for straying from the Covenant. This warning may also apply to other faith groups, like Muslims and Christians, as a general principle of divine justice, so that they may repent, believe and adjust their conduct.

(7:167): "Behold! Your Lord declared (1140) that He would send against them (the Children of Israel), to the Day of Judgment, those who would afflict them with grievous penalty. Your Lord is quick in retribution, but He is also Oft-forgiving, Most Merciful."

"See Deut. 11:28; 'A curse if ye will not obey the commandments of the Lord your God but turn aside out of the way I command you this day'; also Deut. 28:49; 'The Lord shall bring a nation against thee from afar, from the end of the earth, as swift as the eagle flieth; a nation whose tongue thou shalt not understand'; and many other passages." (FN1140)

(7:168): "We broke them up into sections on this earth. (1141) There are among them some that are the righteous, and some that are the opposite. We have tried them with both prosperity and adversity: In order that they might turn (to us)."

"The dispersal of the Jews is a great fact in the world's history. Neither has their persecution ended yet, nor is it likely to end as far as we can foresee." (FN1141)

(7:169): "After them succeeded an (evil) generation: They inherited the Book, but they chose (for themselves) (1142) the vanities of this world, saying (for excuse): "'(Everything) will be forgiven us.' (Even so), if similar vanities came their way, they would (again) seize them. Was not the covenant (1143) of the Book taken from them, that they would not ascribe to God anything but the truth? and they study what is in the Book. But best for the righteous is the home in the Hereafter. Will you not understand?"

"Merely inheriting a Book, or doing lip service to it, does not make a nation righteous. If they succumb to the temptations of the world, their hypocrisy becomes all the more glaring. 'High finance' is one of these temptations. Cf. also 2:80: 'the Fire shall not touch us except for a few numbered days': and 2:88, about their blasphemous self-sufficiency." (FN1142)

"Cf. Exod. 19:5-8; 24:3; 39:27; and many other passages." (FN1143)

(7:170): "As to those who hold fast by the Book and establish regular prayer, - never shall We suffer the reward of the righteous to perish."

Chapter Fifteen - God commands the Children of Israel to believe in Prophet Muhammad

The Qur'an frequently addresses the Children of Israel, urging them to recognise Prophet Muhammad as foretold by earlier prophets, such as Moses and Jesus as mentioned in Verses 7:155-159, 61:6-9, 5:15-16 and 5:19, given below.

I will also refer to several Verses in the Quran which commend the righteous Jews. These are Verses 2:47, 3:75, 3:113-115, 3:199, 7:159 and 7:168.

Verses commanding the Children of Israel to believe in Prophet Muhammad

(7:155): "And Moses chose from his people seventy men for Our appointment. And when the earthquake seized them, he said, 'My Lord, if You had willed, You could have destroyed them before and me [as well]. Would You destroy us for what the foolish among us have done? This is not but Your trial by which You send astray whom You will and guide whom You will. You are our Protector, so forgive us and have mercy upon us; and You are the best of forgivers."

(7:156): "And decree for us in this world [that which is] good and [also] in the Hereafter; indeed, we have turned back to You." [God] said, "My punishment - I

afflict with it whom I will, but My mercy encompasses all things. So I will decree it [especially] for those who fear Me and give zakat and those who believe in Our Signs;"

(7:157): "'Those who follow the Messenger, the unlettered Prophet, whom they find written in what they have of the Torah and the Gospel, who enjoins upon them what is right and forbids them what is wrong and makes lawful for them the good things and prohibits for them the evil and relieves them of their burden and the shackles which were upon them. So they who have believed in him, honoured him, supported him and followed the light which was sent down with him - it is those who will be the successful.'"

(7:158): "Say, [O Muhammad], 'O mankind! indeed I am the Messenger of God to you all, [from Him] to whom belongs the dominion of the heavens and the earth. There is no deity except Him; He gives life and causes death.' So believe in God and His Messenger, the unlettered prophet, who believes in God and His words, and follow him that you may be guided."

(7:159): "And among the people of Moses is a community which guides by truth and by it establishes justice."

In Verse 7:157 above, is a prefiguring, to Moses, of the Arabian Messenger, the last of the Messengers of God. Prophecies about him will be found in the Torah and the Gospel. In the reflex of the Torah as now accepted by the Jews, Moses says: "The Lord thy God will raise up unto thee a Prophet from the midst of thee, of thy brethren, like unto me" (Deut. 18:15): "the only Prophet who brought a Shari'ah like that of Moses was Muhammad, and he came of the house of Isma'il, the brother of Isaac, the father of Israel. In the reflex of the Gospel as now accepted by the Christians, Christ promised another Comforter, (John 14:16): "the Greek word Paraclete which the Christians interpret as referring to the Holy Spirit is by our Doctors of Law taken to be Periclyte, which would be the Greek form of Ahmad. This is mentioned in Verse 61:6 given below.

In Chapter 61 of the Qur'an, Jesus gives the glad tidings of the Ministry of Prophet Muhammad:

(61:6): "And [mention] when Jesus, the son of Mary, said, 'O children of Israel, indeed I am the messenger of God to you confirming what came before me of the Torah and bringing good tidings of a messenger to come after me, whose name is Ahmad.' But when he came to them with clear evidences, they said, 'This is obvious magic.'"

(61:7): "And who is more unjust than one who invents about God untruth while he is being invited to Islam. And God does not guide the wrongdoing people."

(61:8): "They want to extinguish the light of God with their mouths, but God will perfect His light, although the disbelievers dislike it."

(61:9): "It is He who sent His Messenger (Muhammad) with guidance and the religion of truth to manifest it over all religion, although those who associate others with God dislike it."

In Chapter 5 of the Qur'an, God commands both the Jews and the Christians to believe in Muhammad and to follow the Book (the Qur'an), revealed to him:

(5:15): "O People of the Book! There has come to you Our Messenger making clear to you much of what you used to conceal of the Scripture and overlooking much. There has come to you from God a light and a clear Book."

(5:16): "By which God guides those who pursue His pleasure to the ways of peace and brings them out from darknesses into the light, by His permission, and guides them to a straight path."

(5:19): "O People of the Book! There has come to you Our Messenger (Muhammad) to make clear to you [the religion] after a period [of suspension] of messengers, lest you say, 'There came not to us any bringer of good tidings or a warner.' But there has come to you a bringer of good tidings and a warner. And God has power over all things."

Does God commend the righteous Jews?

The answer is yes. There are numerous verses in the Qur'an where God praises the righteous Jews for their good conduct, for example:

(2:47): "O Children of Israel, call to mind My special favour which I bestowed upon you, and that I preferred you to all others."

(3:75): "Among the People of the Book are some who, if entrusted with hoard of gold, will (readily) pay it back; others, who, if entrusted with a single silver coin, will not repay it unless you constantly stood demanding..."

(3:113-115): "Not all of them are alike: Of the People of the Book are a portion that stand (for the right); they rehearse the Revelation of God all night long, and they prostrate themselves in adoration. They believe in God and the Last Day; they enjoin what is right and forbid what is wrong; and they hasten in all good works. They are in the ranks of the righteous. Of the good that they do, nothing will be rejected of them, for God knows well those that they do right."

(3:199): "And there are, certainly, among the People of the Book, those who believe in God, in the Revelation to you, and in the Revelation to them, bowing in humility to God. They will not sell the Revelation of God for a miserable gain. For them is a reward with their Lord, and God is swift in account."

(7:159): "Of the people of Moses there is a section who guide and do justice in the light of truth."

(7:168): "We broke them up into sections on this earth. There are among them some that are the righteous, and some that are the opposite. We have tried them with both prosperity and adversity, in order that they may turn to Us."

Please remember that Prophet Muhammad (pbuh), married a Jewish woman, Sapheia, who was given by God the title of "the Mother of the Believers". His swords were made by a Jew in Medinah. When the Prophet Muhammad (pbuh) died, his shield was mortgaged with a Jew, to show us that among the Jews there are those who abide by God's Commandments and do not take usury.

A chaste Muslim man is permitted to marry a chaste Jewish or Christian woman. She does not have to embrace Islam and will have the same rights as a Muslim wife, as stated in Verse 5:5. The food of the People of the Book is lawful to Muslims and the food of the Muslims is lawful to the people of the Book, again as mentioned in Verse 5:5. Moreover, during periods of persecution in Europe, many Jewish communities found refuge in Muslim lands, where they were often granted safety and religious freedom.

In 2:109 and 3:186, God commands the Muslims to tolerate and forgive insults from the People of the Book.

(2:109): "Many of the People of the Book (Jews and Christians), wish to turn you back into disbelievers after you have accepted the faith, out of their selfish

envy, (even) after the truth has become manifest to them. Yet, pardon and overlook till God brings about His command. Surely, God is powerful over all things."

And He says in verse
(3:186): "You shall certainly be tried and tested in your possessions and in your own selves, and you will surely hear from those who have been given the Book before you (Jews and Christians) and from the idolaters, much that is offensive and hurtful. But if you are patient and fear God, that is the best course."

Islam is a religion of peace, tolerance and justice. It condemns the killing of innocent people anywhere in the world irrespective of their religion or race even if Islam is insulted or ridiculed. Do not blame the Qur'an, blame those who do not understand it among the Muslims and non-Muslims.

Chapter Sixteen - God's punishment of the two Jewish tribes of Banu Al Nadir and Banu Qurayzah in Madinah, during the time of Prophet Muhammad (pbuh)

The Tribe of Banu Al Nadir

In Verses 59:1-7, God tells us how He mildly punished the Jewish Tribe of Banu Al Nadir for their blasphemy.

(59:1): "Whatever is in the heavens and on earth, declares the Praises and Glory (5368) of God. For He is the Exalted in Might, the Wise."

"This verse, introducing the Surah is identical with 57:1, introducing S. 57. The theme of both is the wonderful working of God's Plan and Providence. In the one case it referred to the conquest of Makkah and taught the lesson of humility. In this case it refers to the dislodgement of the treacherous Banu al Nadir from their nest of intrigue in the neighbourhood of Madinah, practically without a blow." (FN5368) See next note.

(59:2): "It is He Who got out the Unbelievers among the People of the Book (5369) from their homes at the first gathering (of the forces). Little did you think that they would get out"
(5370) "And they thought that their fortresses would defend them from God. But the (Wrath of) God came to them from quarters (5371) from which they little

expected (it), and cast terror into their hearts, so that they destroyed their dwellings by their own (5372) hands and the hands of the Believers, take warning, then, O you with eyes (to see)!"

"This refers to the Jewish tribe of Banu al Nadir whose intrigues and treachery nearly undid the Muslim cause during the perilous days of the battle of Uhud in Shawwal, A.H. 3. Four months after, in Rabi' al Awwal, A.H. 4, steps were taken against them. They were asked to leave the strategic position which they occupied, about three miles south of Madinah, endangering the very existence of the Ummah in Madinah. At first, they demurred, relying on their fortresses and on their secret alliances with the Pagans of Makkah and the Hypocrites of Madinah. But when the Muslim army was gathered to punish them and actually besieged them for some days, their allies stirred not a finger in their aid, and they were wise enough to leave. Most of them joined their brethren in Syria, which they were permitted to do, after being disarmed. Some of them joined their brethren in Khaybar: see n. 3705 to 33:27. Banu al Nadir richly deserved punishment, but their lives were spared, and they were allowed to carry away their goods and chattels." (FN5369)

"That is, without actual hostilities, and the shedding of precious Muslim blood." (FN5370)

They had played a double game. Originally, they were sworn allies of the Madinah Muslims under the Prophet, but they secretly intrigued with the Makkah Pagans under Abu Sufyan and the Madinah Hypocrites. They even tried treacherously to take the life of the Prophet while he was on a visit to them, breaking both the laws of hospitality and their own sworn alliance.

"They thought the Pagan Quraysh of Makkah and the Hypocrites of Madinah would help them, but they did not help them. On the contrary the eleven-day siege showed them their own helplessness. Their supplies were cut off: the exigencies of the siege necessitated the destruction of their outlying palm trees; and the unexpected turn in their fortunes disheartened them. Their hearts were struck with terror and they capitulated. But they laid waste their homes before they left: see next note." (FN5371)

"Their lives were spared, and they were allowed ten days in which to remove themselves, their families, and such goods as they could carry. In order to leave no habitations for the Muslims they demolished their own houses and laid waste their property, to complete the destruction which the operations of war had already caused at the hands of the besieging force of the Muslims." (FN5372)

(59:3): "And had it not been that God had decreed banishment for them, (5373) He would certainly have punished them in this world; And in the Hereafter they shall (certainly) have the Punishment of the Fire."

"Banishment was a comparatively mild punishment for them, but the Providence of God had decreed that a chance should be given to them even though they were a treacherous foe. Within two years, their brethren the Banu Qurayzah showed that they had not profited by their example and had to be dealt with in another way: see 33:26 and notes." (FN5373)

(59:4): "That is because they resisted God and His Messenger. and if anyone resists God, (5374) verily God is severe in Punishment."

"The punishment of Banu al Nadir was because in breaking their plighted word with the Messenger and in actively resisting God's Message and supporting the enemies of that Message, they rebelled against His Holy Will. For such treason and rebellion, the punishment is severe, and yet in this case it was seasoned with Mercy." (FN5374).

(59:5): "Whether you cut down (O you Muslims!) The tender palm- trees, or you left them standing on their roots, it was (5375) by leave of God, and in order that He might (5376) cover with shame the rebellious transgressors."

"The unnecessary cutting down of fruit trees or destruction of crops, or any wanton destruction whatever in war, is forbidden by the law and practice of Islam. But some destruction may be necessary for putting pressure on the enemy, and to that extent it is allowed. But as far as possible, consistently with that objective of military operations, such trees should not be cut down. Both these principles are in accordance with the Divine Will and were followed by the Muslims in their expedition." (FN5375)

"The arrogance of Banu al Nadir had to be humbled, and their power for mischief destroyed." (FN5376)

(59:6): "What God has bestowed on His Messenger (and taken away) from them - for this you made no expedition with either cavalry or camelry; (5377) but

215

God gives power to His messengers over any He pleases; and God (5378) has power over all things."

"Neither cavalry nor troops mounted on camels were employed in the siege. In fact, the enemy surrendered at the first onset. See 59:2, and n. 5369 above." (FN5377)

"God accomplishes His Purpose in various ways, according to His Wise and Holy Will and Plan. In some cases, a fight is necessary. In some cases, the godly attain their objective and overawe the forces of evil without actual fighting." (FN5378)

(59:7): "What God has bestowed (5379) on His Messenger (and taken away) from the people (5380) of the townships, belongs to God, to His Messenger (5381) and to kindred and orphans, the needy and the wayfarer; In order that it may not (merely) make a circuit between the wealthy among you. So, take what the Messenger assigns to you, and deny yourselves that which he withholds from you. (5381-A) And fear God. for God is strict in Punishment."

"The Jews had originally come from outside Arabia, and seized on the land near Madinah. They refused to adapt themselves to the people of Arabia, and were in fact a thorn in the side of the genuine Arabs of Madinah. Their dispossession is therefore a restoration of the land to its original people. But the word 'Fai' is here understood in a technical sense, as meaning property abandoned by the enemy or taken from him without a formal war. In that sense it is distinguished from Anfal, or spoils, taken after actual fighting, about which see 8:1- 41." (FN5379)

"The people of the townships": the townships were the Jewish settlements round Madinah, of the Banu al Nadir, and possibly of other tribes. Cf. the "townships" mentioned in 59:14 below. The reference cannot be to Wadi al Qura (Valley of Towns), now Mada'in Salih, which was subjugated after Khaybar and Fadak in A.H. 7, unless this verse is later than the rest of the Surah" (FN5380)

"'Belongs to God': i.e., to God's Cause; and the beneficiaries are further detailed. No shares are fixed; they depend upon circumstances, and are left to the judgement of the Leader. Compare a similar list of those entitled to Charity, in 2:177, but the two lists refer to different circumstances and have different beneficiaries in-addition to the portion common to both." (FN5381)

"Alternatively, these words may be translated: 'So take what the Messenger gives you, and refrain from what he prohibits you'". [Eds.] (FN5381-A)

The Tribe of Banu Qurayzah

Did the Prophet Muhammad commit a war crime against the Jews of Banu Qurayzah?

The slaughter of the men of Banu Qurayzah was shocking to many people who are not familiar with their treason. If it were not mentioned in Verses 33:26-27 of the Holy Qur'an we, as Muslims, would have rejected the story as it contradicts the nature of the Prophet and his teachings.

(33:26-27): "And those of the people (3701) of the Book who aided the (enemies)?God took them down from their strongholds (3702) and cast terror into their hearts, (so that) (3703) some you slew, and some (3704) you made captives. And He (God) made you heirs of their lands, their houses, and their goods, and of a land which you had not frequented (before). And God has power over all things."

"The Jewish tribe of the Banu Qurayzah were counted among the citizens of Madinah and were bound by solemn engagements to help in the defence of the city. But on the occasion of the Confederate siege by the Quraish and their allies they intrigued with the enemies and treacherously aided them. Immediately after the siege was raised and the Confederates had fled in hot haste, the Prophet turned his attention to these treacherous 'friends' who had betrayed his city in the hour of danger. They were filled with terror and dismay when Madinah was free from the Quraish danger. They shut themselves up in their castles and sustained a siege of 25 days, after which they surrendered, stipulating that they would abide by the decision of their fate at the hands of Sa'd Ibn Mu'az, chief

of the Aus tribe, with which they had been in alliance"
(FN3701- FN3702).

It is a known fact that the Jews, at the time of the Prophet, only accepted their own Law. It was the Jews who suggested the appointment of Sa'd Ibn Mu'az as an arbiter. The Prophet accepted their choice. Sa'd applied the Jewish Law of the Old Testament, when he judged in the matter.

Footnotes 3703 and 3704, Chapter 33, of the translation of the Qur'an by Abdullah Yusuf Ali, read: "Saad applied to them the Jewish Law of the Old Testament, not as strictly as the case warranted.
In Deut. 20:10-18, the treatment of a city 'which is very far off from thee' is prescribed to be comparatively more lenient than the treatment of a city 'of the people, which the Lord thy God does give thee for an inheritance', i.e., which is near enough to corrupt the religion of the Jewish people.

"The punishment for these is total annihilation: 'thou shall save alive nothing that breatheth' (Deut. 20:16). The more lenient treatment for far-off cities is described in the next note. According to the Jewish standard, then, the Banu Qurayzah deserved total extermination-of men, women and children. They were in the territory of Madinah itself, and further they had broken their engagements and helped the enemy."

"Saad adjudged them the mildest treatment of the 'far-off' cities which is thus described in the Jewish Law: 'Thou shalt smite every male thereof with the edge of the sword: but the women and the little ones, and the cattle, and all that is in the city, even all the spoil thereof, shalt thou take unto thyself, and thou shalt eat the spoil of thine enemies, which the Lord thy God hath given thee' (Deut. 20:13- 14).

"The men of the Banu Qurayzah were slain: the women were sold as captives of war: and their lands and properties were divided among the Muhajireen."

So, the Prophet Muhammad cannot be accused of committing any war crimes, or as stated by someone, a "holocaust" against the Jews. The punishment was determined by God for their blasphemy.

Chapter Seventeen - Was Balfour antisemitic?

Palestine was part of the Ottoman Empire, which ruled much of the Middle East until the end of World War I. After the defeat of the Ottoman Empire in World War I, Britain took control of Palestine under a League of Nations mandate. Palestine was predominantly inhabited by Arabs, with a Jewish minority and other smaller ethnic groups.

Arthur Balfour, (the nephew of the previous PM, Lord Salisbury), was a prominent figure in British politics and a supporter of Zionist aspirations. He is perhaps best known for authoring the "Balfour Declaration" of 1917, while he was serving as Foreign Secretary. This declaration supported the establishment of a Jewish Homeland in Palestine. On 2nd November 1917, he wrote to Lionel Walter Rothschild who was the figurehead of the British Jewish community and is the man to whom the Declaration was addressed.

"Dear Lord Rothschild,

I have much pleasure in conveying to you, on behalf of His Majesty's Government, the following declaration of sympathy with Jewish Zionist aspirations which has been submitted to, and approved by, the Cabinet.

'His Majesty's Government view with favour the establishment in Palestine of a national home for the Jewish people, and will use their best endeavours to facilitate the achievement of this object, it being clearly

understood that nothing shall be done which may prejudice the civil and religious rights of existing non-Jewish communities in Palestine, or the rights and political status enjoyed by Jews in any other country.'

I should be grateful if you would bring this declaration to the knowledge of the Zionist Federation.

Yours sincerely,

Arthur James Balfour"

In 1922, the League of Nations entrusted Britain with the task of establishing a "national home" for the Jewish people in Palestine. This stemmed from the Balfour Declaration of 1917, a pledge made by the then Foreign Secretary, Arthur Balfour, to Britain's Jewish community. The declaration was enshrined in the British mandate over Palestine. The Palestinians felt that they had been betrayed by Britain and this led to growing tensions between the Jewish and Arab populations.

Many Arab and Muslim politicians believe that Balfour's promise, not only harmed the Palestinians, but also betrayed the Jews. In fact, they regard him as "antisemitic!". The same view was attributed to Lord William Peel, who chaired the "Royal Palestinian Commission", in 1936.

Following the "Arab Revolt" In 1936, the British Government established, the "Peel Commission", officially known as the "Palestine Royal Commission", as a British investigative body to address the escalating unrest in Mandatory Palestine.

Its primary objective was to examine the underlying causes of the Arab Revolt (1936–1939) and propose potential solutions to the ongoing conflict between Jews and Arabs in the region. Here is a comprehensive overview of the Peel Commission and its significance:

Background:

- After World War I, Britain assumed control of Palestine under a League of Nations mandate, with a dual responsibility to establish a Jewish national home (as per the Balfour Declaration of 1917) and safeguard the civil and religious rights of the Arab inhabitants.
- In the 1920s and 1930s, a surge in Jewish immigration and land acquisitions led to mounting Arab resentment and violent clashes.
- The Arab Revolt (1936–1939) was a significant nationalist uprising by Palestinian Arabs against British rule and Jewish immigration, prompting Britain to dispatch the Peel Commission.

Formation and Objectives:

- The Peel Commission was established in 1936 under the leadership of Lord William Peel by the British government.
- Its primary objectives were to investigate the causes of unrest, assess the effectiveness of the Mandate, and recommend future political arrangements.

Key Findings of the Commission (1937 Report):

The commission concluded that the conflicting aspirations of Jews and Arabs in Palestine were fundamentally irreconcilable under a single state solution. The Mandate system, they argued, had become unworkable and failed to maintain peace or satisfy either community.

The Peel Commission proposed the partition of Palestine into two separate states: a Jewish state in the north and along the Mediterranean coast, and an Arab state in the remainder of the territory, linked to Transjordan. Jerusalem and surrounding areas would remain under British control as an international zone due to their religious significance.

The Jewish state would comprise about 20% of Palestine but would include most of the Jewish population. The Arab state would be larger but more rural and less economically developed. The commission controversially suggested a voluntary (and if necessary, compulsory) transfer of Arabs from the proposed Jewish state.

The Zionist/Jewish response was mixed but largely positive. Zionist leaders, including David Ben-Gurion, saw it as a historic opportunity to gain recognised sovereignty. Some were disappointed with the size of the proposed Jewish state but supported partition as a step forward.

The Arab/Palestinian response was vehemently opposed. They rejected the idea of any Jewish state or further Jewish immigration. They demanded independence for all of Palestine and an end to the Mandate and Jewish immigration.

The outcome of the partition led to the creation of Israel in 1948 and the displacement of hundreds of thousands of Palestinians. The legacy of the partition continues to be a source of conflict and tension in the region.

The British government initially accepted the concept of partition in principle and planned a follow-up technical survey, known as the Woodhead Commission (1938). However, due to strong Arab opposition, practical challenges, and the deteriorating international situation, the British had abandoned the partition plan by 1939.

Instead, Britain issued the 1939 White Paper, which severely restricted Jewish immigration—a move that deeply angered the Zionist movement, particularly on the eve of the Holocaust.

The Peel Commission was the first official recommendation of partition as a solution to the conflict in Palestine. It established a precedent for future partition proposals, including the UN Partition Plan of 1947 (Resolution 181).

Furthermore, the commission underscored the deep-seated nature of the Jewish-Arab conflict and the limitations of colonial governance in addressing nationalist aspirations.

Why do most Arabs and Jews regard Balfour and Peel as being antisemitic?

Let me answer this question. The Christian West had persecuted their local Jewish communities periodically through history, well before the first and second World Wars. In the Middle Ages, antisemitism in Europe was framed in religious terms. Many Christians, including members of the clergy, held the Jewish people collectively responsible for the killing of Jesus. According to this interpretation, both the Jews present at Jesus Christ's death and the Jewish people collectively and for all time, have committed the sin of god-killing (deicide). For 1900 years of Christian-Jewish history, the charge of god-killing has led to hatred, violence against and murder of Jews in Europe and America.

Between the 1920s and 1940s, the number of Jews arriving in Palestine grew, with many fleeing from persecution in Europe, especially the Nazi Holocaust in World War Two. The arrival of Jews in large numbers increased violence between Jews and Arabs, and against British rule.

In 1947, the UN voted for Palestine to be split into separate Jewish and Arab states, with Jerusalem becoming an international city. That plan was accepted by Jewish leaders but rejected by the Arab side and never implemented.

The Christian West created the State of Israel in Palestine in the full knowledge that: the neighbouring Arab States, who had bravely fought against Western Imperialism, would not accept it; and that the Jews living in the State of

Israel would never experience peace or security. The Christian West did this out of antisemitism and not out of love for the Jewish people.

In 1948, unable to solve the problem, Britain withdrew and Jewish leaders declared the creation of the State of Israel. It was intended to be a safe haven for Jews fleeing persecution, as well as a national homeland for Jews. Sadly, fighting between Jewish and Arab militias had been intensifying for months, and the day after Israel declared statehood, five Arab countries attacked. Hundreds of thousands of Palestinians fled or were forced out of their homes in what they call Al-Nakba, or the "Catastrophe".

By the time the fighting ended in a ceasefire the following year, Israel controlled most of the territory. Jordan occupied land which became known as the West Bank, and Egypt occupied Gaza. Jerusalem was divided between Israeli forces in the West, and Jordanian forces in the East. The Arab States have been in constant wars with Israel since its forced formation in 1948, due to the nonexistence of a peace agreement.

The Christian West created the State of Israel in order to serve its own interests, mainly to create instability in the region, to sell arms and exert influence over the Arab States to control and oppress its people and rob their natural resources. It was a form of colonisation. In doing that, they had no consideration for the innocent Jewish and Arab lives which would be lost. The entire agenda was not only "antisemitic", but "antihuman".

When the persecuted, vulnerable, fearful Jews fled the Nazi persecution in Europe, they were only offered passage to Palestine, which had been decided by Balfour in 1917, long before the first and second World Wars. The colonial nation that Balfour represented did not own the land of Palestine and thus had no standing to gift it to another people. Not only that, but also the British never honoured the commitment made by Balfour in his declaration stating that: *"it being clearly understood that nothing shall be done which may prejudice the civil and religious rights of existing non-Jewish communities in Palestine".*

In the USA, the Christian Zionist movement and Christians United for Israel (CUFI), who mainly comprise of white evangelical Protestants, support Jews worldwide to settle in Israel. They believe that by massing the Jews in Israel, the return of Jesus would be accelerated. This is a very selfish and antisemitic approach, as they have no regard for the sacrifices these innocent Jews would make by settling in Israel.

The historical record shows that Muslim Empires, including the Ottoman Empire, never persecuted the Jews. On the contrary, they provided safe havens for them when the Christian West persecuted them. It's important to note that Jews lived in Palestine in total harmony with Muslims and Christians, long before Israel. If the Christian West genuinely cared about the safety and prosperity of the Jewish people, it would have enabled them to stay as citizens of the countries they were already settled in. It has also been argued that the establishment of Israel in a location other than Palestine, such as California or Uganda as originally intended, may have offered a safer and more prosperous alternative for the Jewish population.

God said to David in Verse 38:2 in the Qur'an: "O David, We have appointed you vicegerent on earth. Therefore, rule among people with justice and do not follow (your) desire lest it should lead you astray from God's Path. God's severe punishment awaits those who stray away from God's Path, for they had forgotten the Day of Reckoning."

Unfortunately, Balfour and his clan forgot the Day of Reckoning! If there is no justice, there will be no peace.

Chapter Eighteen - Is Israel an occupier?

Very often, you may hear some politicians claiming that Israel is an occupier. The State of Israel was formally established by the Israeli Declaration of Independence on 14th May 1948. The U.S. President Harry S. Truman recognised the new nation on the same day. Israel was admitted to the United Nations (UN) as a full member state on 11th May 1949, with very well defined and recognised borders.

Between 5th June and 10th June 1967 Israel defeated Egypt, Jordan, and Syria and occupied the Sinai Peninsula, the Gaza Strip, the West Bank, East Jerusalem, and the Golan Heights. From the beginning, the United States sought a ceasefire in order to prevent an Arab defeat bad enough to force the Soviet Union to intervene. I personally witnessed this war as I was at my final year at Cairo University in Egypt.

On 22nd November 1967, the United Nations Security Council issued Resolution 242 commanding Israel to withdraw from all occupied territories. Unfortunately, Israel did not comply with this resolution. Following the disgraceful defeat of the Arab armies, late President Naser of Egypt said: "Whatever was taken by force can only be restored by force". This is in accordance with international law, and the UN Charter.

I recently came across a very interesting discussion which took place between the late King Faisal of Saudi Arabia and Charles de Gaulle, the late French President, which I give below.

"Poor Paris, I don't know Who it will belong to...!"

This is a sentence pronounced by King Faisal bin Abdul Aziz to the French President Charles de Gaulle.

Dr. Maʿrouf al-Dawalibi, in his memoirs, reports this important exchange between King Faisal bin Abdul Aziz and President Charles de Gaulle.

Here is a summary of the dialogue that took place:

De Gaulle said:
"Your Majesty, we hear speeches claiming that you want to throw ISRAEL into the Sea. ISRAEL is now a reality, and no one in the world will agree to change this state of affairs."

King Faisal replied:
"Mr. President, I am surprised by your words. Hitler occupied Paris, and this has become a fait accompli. All of France surrendered, except you. You withdrew with the British army and continued to resist this state of affairs until you triumphed. You did not accept the imposed reality, and neither did your people. I am therefore surprised that you ask me today to accept a fait accompli.
Woe, Mr. President, to the Weak if he submits to the Strong."

(During this exchange, King Faisal mentioned General de Gaulle's principle:

"An occupation that becomes a fait accompli cannot become legitimate.")

De Gaulle, surprised by the King's liveliness of mind, changes his tone and says:
"Your Majesty, the JEWS say that Palestine is their land of origin, and that their ancestor ISRAEL was born there."

King Faisal replies:
"Mr. President, I admire you because you are a religious and believing man. You certainly read the BIBLE.

Have you not read that the Jews came from Egypt as invaders, that they burned the cities, and Killed men, women and children?

How can you say that Palestine is their land when it belongs to the Arab Canaanites?

The Jews were colonisers.

You want to restore a 4,000 year old colonisation carried out by Israel. Why then not restore the Colonisation of France by Rome, which dates back only 3,000 years?

Should we redraw the Map of the WORLD for the benefit of the Jews and not for the benefit of Rome?

We, the Arabs, spent 2 Centuries in the South of France, while the Jews spent only 70 years in Palestine, before being Exiled. "

De Gaulle answers:
"But they say that their father was born there."

King Faisal retorts:
"Amazing... You currently have 150 Embassies in Paris, and many ambassadors have children who were born there. If these children later become heads of state and claim Paris as their birthright, then poor Paris, I don't know to whom it will belong...!"

De Gaulle, silent, rings a bell and brings in Georges Pompidou, then Prime Minister, who was with Prince Sultan and Rachad Farhan.

De Gaulle then declares:
"Now I have understood the Palestinian question. Stop exporting arms to Israel." (At the time, Israel was still fighting with French weapons, not American ones).

Dr. al-Dawalibi continues:
"We welcomed King Faisal to Dhahran on his return from this meeting. The next morning, the King summoned the Chairman of the American Tapline Oil Company, and I witnessed this conversation.

The King said:
"Any drop of oil that goes to Israel will result in a total stoppage of our exports to you."
When the King learned that the United States had sent aid to Israel, he suspended the supply of oil, causing protests in America. People lined up in front of gas stations, chanting: "We want oil, not Israel!"

Source:
Memoirs of Maʿrouf al-Dawalibi,former Prime Minister of Syria in 1953, was born in Aleppo in 1907 and died in

Medina in 2004. He was buried in the Baqī' Cemetery. He is the author of more than 10 books on Islam.

This is why King Faisal was assassinated. May God have mercy on him and accept him as a Martyr among the great people of the Arab and Islamic Nations.

Thus, the occupier must be fought as Europe fought against German occupation in the First World War and Nazi occupation in the Second World War.

On 6th October 1973, late President Sadat of Egypt, waged a successful war against Israel, to restore the occupied territories. He liberated Sinai and restored navigation in Suez Canal. Later in 1978 he signed a peace treaty with Israel. Israel withdrew from Gaza in September 2005 and imposed a blockade on it. The Golan Heights, the West Bank, and East Jerusalem continue to be under Israeli occupation. Israel annexed East Jerusalem and the Golan Heights and continues to build illegal settlements in the West Bank, which is against International Law. That is why Israel is referred to by many politicians as an "occupier".

Most Palestinian refugees and their descendants live in Gaza and the West Bank, as well as in neighbouring Jordan, Syria and Lebanon. Neither they nor their descendants have been allowed by Israel to return to their homes - Israel says this would overwhelm the country and threaten its existence as a Jewish state. There are so many UN Security Council Resolutions which Israel has not complied with, relying on the military support and economic assistance it gets from the USA and European countries. Moreover, Israel-Palestinian peace talks were held on and off between the 1990s and 2010s, interspersed with outbreaks of violence.

A negotiated peace did seem possible in the early days. A series of secret talks in Norway became the Oslo peace process, forever symbolised by a ceremony on the White House lawn in 1993 presided over by President Bill Clinton and attended by Yasir Arafat and Yitzhak Rabin.

In a historic moment, the Palestinians recognised the State of Israel and Israel recognised its historical enemy, the Palestine Liberation Organisation (PLO), as the sole representative of the Palestinian people. A self-governing Palestinian Authority was set up.

Cracks soon appeared, though, with then opposition leader Benjamin Netanyahu calling Oslo a mortal threat to Israel. The Israelis accelerated their project to settle Jews in the occupied Palestinian territories. Following Palestinian elections, the militant group Hamas won the election in Gaza against the PLO. Hamas sent suicide bombers to kill people in Israel and wreck the chances of a deal. The atmosphere in Israel turned ugly, culminating in Israeli Prime Minister Yitzhak Rabin's assassination by a Jewish extremist on 4th November 1995. In the 2000s attempts were made to revive the peace process - including in 2003 when a roadmap was devised by world powers with the ultimate goal of a two-state solution, but this was never implemented.

Peace efforts finally stalled in 2014, when talks failed between the Israelis and Palestinians in Washington. The most recent peace plan - prepared by the US when Donald Trump was president - was called "the deal of the century" by Prime Minister Netanyahu,but was dismissed by the Palestinians as one-sided and never got off the ground.

Recently, I watched a video clip of the Israeli journalist Gideon Levy, speaking at the National Press Club, Washington DC, USA. He was condemning the extremely hostile Israeli attitude towards anyone who would not agree with their policies. In the video he humorously and sarcastically unveiled the excuses made to justify their practices.

He said: "......If we are the chosen people, who are you to tell us what to do? Who are you? Who is the international community to tell Israel what to do? International law? Wonderful thing. It doesn't apply on us. It applies on any other place on earth, not on Israel. Because we are the chosen people, don't you understand it? The second very deep-rooted value is obviously the value of we the victims, not only the biggest victims, but the only victims around. I know many occupations which were longer than the Israeli occupation, some were even more brutal, even though it's getting harder and harder to be more brutal than the Israeli occupation. I don't recall one occupation in which the occupier presents himself as the victim. Not only the victim, the only victim. If to phrase here, if to quote here the late Golda Meir, whom I quoted also last time, I know, but it is so unforgettable I have to use it again. She once said that 'we will never forgive the Arabs for forcing us to kill their children'. We are the victims. We are forced to kill their children. Poor us. And as the victim and the only victim in history, again, it enables us the rights to do whatever we want, and nobody is going to tell us what to do because we are the only victims. To this, there is a third, very deep-rooted value, And this is the very deep belief, again, *everyone will deny it, but if you scratch under the skin of almost every Israeli, you'll find it there. The Palestinians are not equal human beings like us. They are not like us. They don't love their children like us. They don't love life like us. They were born to kill. They are cruel. They are sadists. They have no values, no manners. Look how they kill us. This is very, very deep-rooted in Israeli society, and maybe that's the key issue. Because as long as this continues, nothing will move. As long as most of the Israelis don't perceive the Palestinians as equal human beings, we are so much better than them. We are so much developed than them. And we are so much human than them. As long as this is the case, all our dreams, and we have some dreams, and I'll get to them, all our dreams will never become true as long as this core issue will not change."*

Levy, a writer for Israel's Haaretz newspaper, is one of the few voices in his country opposing the occupation and describing Israel as a *"racist regime."* For about 40 years, Levy, who has been personally following the events in the occupied West Bank as a journalist in the field, believes that Israeli society and government are currently in an *"extremely radical state of mind."* He has been a lone voice in telling his readers the truth about what goes on in the Occupied Territories. Is he the most hated man in Israel or the most heroic?

I personally have many Jewish friends who share the same views as Levy. What does God say about them in the Qur'an? He says in
Verse
(7:159): **"And among the people of Moses is a community which guides by truth and by it establishes justice."**

Many European and Arab politicians have recently stated that there will be no peace in the region and Israel will never feel safe if it does not end the occupation, stop the building of illegal settlements and accept the two state solution.

The United Nations General Assembly (UNGA) had overwhelmingly adopted a resolution, on 19th September 2024, calling on Israel to end its illegal occupation of the Palestinian territories within a year, a move that Palestine hailed as *"historic"*. The UNGA demanded that *"Israel brings to an end without delay its unlawful presence in the Occupied Palestinian Territory, which constitutes a wrongful act of a continuing character entailing its international responsibility and do so no later than 12 months"*.

It also called on Israel to make reparations to Palestinians for damages incurred by the occupation. The resolution backed an advisory opinion by the International Court of Justice (ICJ) – the UN's top court – which found that Israel's presence in the Palestinian territories is unlawful and must end. The court ruled in July 2024, that Israel is abusing its status as an occupying power, stressing that Israeli settlements in the West Bank and East Jerusalem are illegal. Unfortunately, Israel continues to show no respect to the UN, the international body which created it.

On 29th December 2024, former President Jimmy Carter passed away at the age of 100. As the 39th president of the United States and as a private citizen, Carter was an advocate for peace between nations, democracy and various humanitarian and environmental causes. But in the Middle East, he is going to be remembered as the father of Arab-Israeli normalisation.

Sad to say that the world lacks quality rulers like late President Sadat of Egypt, late King Faisal of Saudi Arabia, late Prime Minister Isaac Rabin of Israel and late USA President Jimmy Carter. The first three lost their lives trying to achieve lasting peace in the Middle East. They all knew that forced peace without justice for the Palestinians is not true peace and it will not last.

On 8th January 2025, European officials warned Donald Trump against threatening *"sovereign borders"* after the US President-elect refused to rule out military action to seize Greenland. The rebukes on Wednesday were led by German Chancellor Olaf Scholz who said *"the principle of inviolability of borders applies to every country, no matter how powerful."* He added Trump's statements a day earlier had sparked *"notable incomprehension"* among other European Union leaders he had spoken with.

"Borders must not be moved by force. This principle applies to every country, whether in the East or the West," Scholz later wrote on X.

France's foreign minister, Jean-Noel Barrot, also weighed in on Wednesday, 8th January saying Greenland was *"European territory"* and there was *"no question of the EU letting other nations in the world, whoever they may be ... attack its sovereign borders"*

The question I pose to some of the EU leaders is, why do you not speak out against the occupation by Israel of Arab lands following the war on 6th June 1967? Don't you think that your principles should apply equally to every country in the world as you stated above? There are many lessons to learn from past and current wars to ensure our future peace.

God only permits war in self-defence, and under well-defined, strict limits. These limits must not be transgressed: non-combatant civilians including women, children and old and infirm men should not be molested, nor trees and crops cut down, nor peace withheld when the enemy comes to terms.

God says in Verse
(2:190): " Fight in the cause of God those who fight you, but don't transgress limits, for God doesn't love transgressors."

And He says in Verse
(22:40): "....Had not God repelled one set of people by means of another there would surely have been pulled down monasteries, churches, synagogues, and mosques, in which the name of God is commemorated in abundant measure. God will certainly give victory to those who aid His cause, for verily God is Full of Strength, Exalted in Might."

God also promotes peace and reconciliation and encourages the parties at war to do that. He says in Verse *(8:61): "But if the enemy inclines towards peace, you should also incline towards peace, and trust in God, for He is the one that hears and knows all things."*

While we must always be ready for the good fight lest it be forced on us, even in the midst of the fight we must always be ready for peace if there is any inclination towards peace on the other side. There is no merit merely for a fight itself. It should be a joyful duty not for itself, but to establish the reign of peace, righteousness and God's Moral Law.

God promises those who were killed while fighting in His cause great reward in the Hereafter.
He says in Verses
(3:169-170): "Don't regard those who are slain in God's way as dead. No, they live, finding their sustenance in the presence of their Lord. They rejoice in the bounty provided by God, and with regard to those left behind, who have not yet joined them in their bliss, they glory in the fact that on them is no fear, nor have they cause to grieve."

Chapter Nineteen - The war on Gaza and the Israeli-Palestinian Conflict

The terrorist attack on Israel by Hamas, on 7th October 2023 and the disproportionate military response by Israel on Gaza, shocked the entire world and led South Africa and other countries to take the case to the International Court of Justice (ICJ), accusing the Israeli government of committing war crimes and genocide against the Palestinian people. Karim Khan, the Prosecutor of the International Criminal Court (ICC), sought arrest warrants for leaders of both Israel and Hamas. On 21st November 2024 arrest warrants were issued for Netanyahu, Gallant and the Hamas commander over alleged war crimes.

The reason I referred to the attack by Hamas as a "terrorist attack" is because the most prominent Islamic scholar in Gaza has issued a rare, powerful fatwa condemning Hamas' 7 October 2023 attack on Israel, which triggered the devastating war in the Palestinian territory. The fatwa is given at the end of this chapter.
God refers in Verse 2:74 in the Quran, that the hearts of those who blasphemed from the Children of Israel became harder than rocks.

(2:74): "Then your hearts became hardened after that, being like rocks or even harder. For indeed, there are rocks from which rivers burst forth, and there are some of them that split open and water comes out, and there are some of them that fall down for fear of God. And God is not unaware of what you do."

I could not imagine that anything could be harder than rocks, until we all witnessed the brutal, inhumane, ruthless attacks on non-combatant civilians, especially the children and women in Gaza. Many Western countries which, not only promote freedom of speech, democracy, human rights, civil liberties and justice for all, but also force these values on other countries, were the first countries to silence and punish anyone who was calling for a cease fire or condemning the killing of innocent civilians in Gaza by Israel.

The peaceful marches were described as "hate marches" and many university students and eminent academics were arrested and detained. This showed the double standards and the hypocrisy of those Western countries who forgot that there is a Just God who is watching over us all. They forgot that there will be a Day of Judgment and life after death. They forgot how God dealt with tyranny in the past. Many nations and civilisations came and went and became tales of the past, because they ignored God's Moral Law.

I quote below a few paragraphs from the article by Robert Crux | 2 November 2023 | (Collateral Damage: A Primer on Evangelicals, Israel, and the War for the Holy Land – Adventist Today)

"The Israel-Hamas war:
In the current turmoil threatening stability in the Middle East, many Bible commentators are speculating that the Jewish temple could be rebuilt in the months and years to come. The construction of the third temple and restoration

*of temple sacrifices will signal the start of the final events
of earth's history.*

*For evangelicals and Zionists, it is advantageous for Israel
to win the current war, eradicating Hamas and bringing the
construction of the third temple closer to reality. Sarah
Posner, a columnist for MSNBC reminds us that for these
evangelicals, "What happens to the Jews and Palestinians
is, to put it very mildly, collateral damage."*

*Christian Zionists are anticipating, and hoping for a war to
end all wars, and a resulting Christian world that they claim
will vanquish evil and bring peace. Only those who accept
Jesus as their saviour will benefit from these events that
Christian Zionists claim the Bible predicts will happen.
Nonbelievers—including Jews and Muslims—will not
survive them.*

*It must be understood that hiding behind evangelical
support for Israel is an authoritarian Christian nationalist
ideology that God is about to force the whole world to
become Christian, and they are leading that charge. God
will bless their efforts to Christianise the world, and the
Israel-Hamas War is just part of the process.*

*And sadly, what happens to real people in the real world
right now really doesn't matter very much to them at all."*

Reflecting on what is said above; reinforces my claim that
the Christian West, led by the Protestant Evangelicals,
continues to be antisemitic and will never give up the
persecution of the Jews even if they use different nations
to carry out their own plans.

My Statement on 13th October 2023

I give below the Statement I read out at our mosque, at the beginning of the Friday sermon on 13th October 2023, which is available on our YouTube channel

"I will say a few words about recent events in Gaza and the Holy Land of which we are all aware, saddened and appalled.
We oppose the killing of non-combatant civilians in Israel and Palestine and other conflicts around the world, irrespective of their religion or ethnicity or race. Likewise, we strongly and wholeheartedly condemn and oppose the mass killing and life changing injuries of Palestinians in Gaza. We pray for the victims in Gaza. I will be offering a funeral prayer after the Friday prayer.
As we did recently for the disasters in Libya and Morocco, we will collect money to alleviate the suffering of those in Gaza. Once the blockade ends, we will send the funds to reputable charities working in Gaza to support the victims. Finally, and especially at this moment, please remember that foreign policy can only be changed by lobbying your MPs and through peaceful and lawful demonstrations and petitions and not through any form of violence as this is against the teachings of Islam and also against the law."

I give below the "Transcript" of my sermon on Friday 20th October 2023, which was disliked by the National Secular Society (NSS), who consequently reported me to the Charity Commission.

Video: How does God deal with the oppressors?

"Salam my dear brothers and sisters, my dear children and grandchildren. Today I'm going to talk about how God deals with the oppressors.

We've been witnessing so many of them in the last few days. I'm not here today to comment on any provoking or intimidating statements made by Israel or any of its supporters, or to quote any empty declarations issued by useless and impotent Muslim and Arab leaders. I will only quote from the Qur'an what God is saying about His wrath which will soon visit the oppressors and their supporters.

Unfortunately, we live in a secular world where the majority of the people don't believe in God. Secular nations only believe in their might and main. They rely entirely on their arsenal of weapons of mass destruction to demoralise, oppress, and exploit the weak and the needy. With their double standards, they practice hypocrisy, not democracy. They have no respect for human lives, blinded by their arrogance and greed. They don't believe that one day they will be held accountable by the Lord of the Worlds for their crimes against humanity.

But those who believe in God and the Hereafter and are courageously fighting the occupiers to liberate their land will prevail by the help of God. The Palestinians will prevail as Moses and the children of Israel prevailed against Pharaoh, and David against Goliath.

God Subhanahu wa Ta'ala says in Verse 111 of Chapter 9:
'God has bought from the believers their lives and possessions in return for Paradise. They fight in the way of God and slay and are slain. It is a promise binding upon Him in the Torah, the Gospel, and the Quran. And who fulfils His covenant better than God? Rejoice then in the bargain that you have made with Him, for that is the mighty triumph.'

God commands in Verse 74 of Chapter 4 that people must defend their countries and fight the occupier, as Europe did in the first and second world wars in their struggle against Nazi aggression and occupation. God says: **"Let those who seek the Hereafter in exchange for the life of this world fight in the way of God, We shall grant a mighty reward to whoever fights in the way of God, whether he is slain or comes out victorious."**

And in Verse 75 of Chapter 4, God commands the defending of those who are weak and oppressed. **"How is it that you don't fight in the way of God and in support of the helpless men, women, and children who pray: 'Our Lord, bring us out of this land whose people are oppressors, and appoint for us from Yourself a protector and appoint for us from Yourself a helper?"** *That was Verse 75 of Chapter 4.*

This is the cry of the innocent victims in Gaza, unfortunately falling on the deaf ears of a blind world. We have all failed, we have all failed them, and God's wrath will encompass all of us.

In Verse 76 of Chapter 4, God commands the fighting of Satan's allies: **"Those who have faith fight in the way of God, while those who disbelieve fight in the way of Satan. Fight, then, against the friends of Satan. Surely Satan's strategy is weak."**

For Muslim countries producing oil and gas they could have at least turned off the taps, as did the late brave Saudi King Faisal in October 1973, may God bless his soul. But the seats of the Muslim leaders are more precious than the blood of the innocent Palestinian children.

British Muslims did condemn the killing of non-combatant civilians in Israel. Did British Jews condemn the killing of innocent civilians in Gaza?

Muslims never persecuted the Jews; on the contrary, they protected them and provided safe haven for them. It was the Christians at the time of the Spanish Inquisition and the Christian Nazi Germany who persecuted the Jews.

In the year 1218, King Henry III of England proclaimed the Edict of the badge, requiring Jews to wear a marking badge. Taxation grew increasingly intense between 1219 and 1272, 49 levies were imposed on Jews for a total of 200,000 marks, a vast sum of money. They were entitled to earn a living as tradesmen or farmers but were not allowed to be part of guilds or to own farmland.

The Jews became poor, and the King could no longer collect taxes from them. Many hundreds were arrested, hanged, and imprisoned, and then, finally, in the year 1290, they were banished from England altogether.

Why would the innocent Palestinians be punished for crimes committed by King Henry III or Queen Isabella or Hitler?

I say to all Western and Muslim leaders what Prophet Lot said to his own people in Verse 78, Chapter 11: **"Is there not even one right-minded person or a single upright leader among you?"**

Shame on all of you. There's a very important factor which all the enemies of the Palestinians ignore: that it is the existence of God, the Almighty, in whom the Palestinians put their full trust.

God says in Verses 173 and 174 of Chapter 3: "Those to whom people said, 'Surely the people have gathered against you **in large numbers, so fear them.' But this threat only increased them in their faith, and they said, 'God is sufficient for us, and an excellent guardian is He.' So, they turned with a mighty favour and a great bounty from God, having suffered no harm. They followed the good pleasure of God, and God is the Lord of great bounty."**

Hasbuna Allah wa Ni'ma Al-Wakeel (God is sufficient for us, and an excellent guardian is He). *That's exactly what the Palestinians are saying, and we are all saying the same.*

There are many verses in the Qur'an telling us how God deals with the oppressors. So let me give you a few examples, starting from Surat Fussilat, Chapter 41. During the time of the Prophet 'Salla Allahu Alayhi Wa Sallam', the

Qur'an came to warn Quraish and gave them the history of those who came before them and resisted their prophets and the destruction they faced at the end. The people God refers to were the people of Ad, Thamud and Pharaoh.

Ad was a tribe which was established immediately after Noah in southern Arabia. They were very powerful, very strong. Their buildings were very tall; they had so many tall pillars. They were themselves very tall people. They were tyrants. Listen to what God says about them, starting from Verse 13 of Chapter 41: **"If your people turn away, O Muhammad, say to them, 'I have warned you of a thunderbolt like the Thunderbolt of Ad and Thamud.'"**

The prophet who came to Ad was Prophet Hud, and the prophet who went to Thamud was Prophet Salih.

(41:14): "Behold, the messengers came to them from before them and behind them, preaching, 'Serve none but God.' They said, 'If our Lord had so pleased, He would certainly have sent down angels, so we disbelieve in the message you were sent with.'"

So, they denied the message with which the Prophet Hud brought to them. What does God say about them in Verse 15? Listen very carefully, please, to what they said and what the enemies of humanity today are saying, exactly the same: **"As for Ad, they behaved arrogantly. They behaved arrogantly through the land against all truth and reason and said: 'Who is superior to us in strength? Who is mightier than we in power?' And God says, 'What! did they not see that God, who created**

250

them, was superior to them in strength and power, was mightier than they in power?' But they continued to reject our signs."

So, they were claiming they are so strong and powerful, and nobody can face them.

And God describes something about their misconduct in Verse 130 of Chapter 26: **When their Prophet Hud said to them: "When you strike, you strike like tyrants, without any responsibility or consideration for those who come within your power."**

Very similar to what we are witnessing now, exactly the same. **"When you lay hands upon anyone, you do so as tyrants. When you strike, you strike with might and main; you are so ruthless."**

What did God do?

"So we sent against them a furious wind through days of disaster, that we might give them a taste of a punishment of humiliation in this life, but the penalty of the Hereafter will be more humiliating still, and they will find no help." 41:16

So, this tribe of Ad and God refers to their city, Iram, that which had so many tall pillars, great temples, and buildings. And God says no other town or city ever being created on this planet like the town or the city of Iram. Where are they today? Gone.

The next one was Thamud, the north of Arabia. You still can see their houses being carved into the rocks of the mountains, known as the "Cities of Saleh". And God Subhanahu wa Ta'ala says: **"As to Thamud, we gave them guidance, but they preferred blindness of heart to guidance, so the thunderbolt of the punishment of humiliation seized them because of what they had earned. But we delivered those who believed and practiced righteousness." 41:17-18**

And in Surat Al-Fajr, Chapter 89, a warning, a reminder, God Subhanahu wa Ta'ala is saying: **"Oh Muhammad, you haven't seen how did God deal with the tribe of the city of Iram with lofty pillars, the like of which has never been created in any other town on Earth, and with Thamud, the people who cut out huge rocks in the valley? How did God deal with Pharaoh of the pyramids?"**

All Ad, Thamud, Pharaoh and the current oppressors, we can see the 27 EU countries and Israel and the USA, all those are oppressors. And God is warning them here. He's saying to them: **"Those who transgressed beyond bounds in the land and heaped therein mischief on mischief. Therefore, your Lord poured on them every type of punishment, for your lord is watchful." 89:11-14**

The three examples given, the Ad, Thamud and Pharaoh, show that neither nations nor individuals, however mighty, prosperous, or firmly established they may be, can live if they transgress the law of God. Just as simple as that, the *law of God, which is also the law of the higher nature which He has bestowed on us, made them in the first place great and glorious. When they fell from it and heaped mischief on mischief, they were swept away. Even though God's punishment is delayed, remember this: God gives respite but God never neglects. Even though God's punishment is delayed, it is not to be supposed that He does not see all things. God's providence is vigilant; his punishment of evildoers is a form of justice to the weak and the righteous whom they oppress. It is part of the signification of his title as Rab, Lord.*

In Surat Yunus, Chapter 10, God tells us the fate of Pharaoh and his hosts in Verse 90: **"We took the children of Israel across the sea, but Pharaoh and his hosts followed them in insolence and spite. When now he was drowning, he said, 'Now I believe that there is no God except Him whom the Children of Israel believe in. I am of those who submit to God in Islam.'"**

What did God say to him? **"Now, but a little while before, you were in rebellion and you did mischief and violence. Today, we save you in the body that you may be a sign to those who come after you. Unfortunately, many among mankind are heedless of our signs." 10:91-92**

He is in the Egyptian Museum, discovered in the year 1881, the mummy of Ramesses the Second. This verse was revealed over 1,400 years ago, but nobody reflects on it as God says.

Does anybody reflect on that when they are slaughtering innocent people for no crime committed by them directly?

Now, I'm going to talk about a very famous battle that happened after the time of Prophet Moses when the Children of Israel were living in the Holy Land. When they ignored the Torah, the teachings of the Torah, God sent so many enemies on them. God sent a prophet called Samuel to them, and they went to him and said, "Why don't you appoint a king to lead us to victory, to fight against the oppressor Goliath and his army, Jalut?" He told them God has chosen a king called Talut, King Saul, and they objected, saying, "No, no, no, he is very poor, from a very poor tribe. He hasn't got enough wealth. No justification that God would appoint such a man. We have more right to lead than him." So, a sign was given to appoint this king. The prophet said God chose him because he has more physical strength and knowledge in how to conduct a war.

The army was formed by King Saul, and I'm going to read to you what exactly happened with this army. How many people disobeyed the leader, how many people managed to fight against Goliath, and what was the end result. So, listen very carefully; this story is very important to reflect on because this is exactly what's happening now. Starting from Verse 249 in Chapter 2, Talut had a huge army of Bani Israel, and now he is marching in the desert.

People were very tired and thirsty, and he had to put them to a test to see how powerful, how patient they are going to persevere in the face of Goliath and his mighty army. So he said, "We are going to come to a river now. If any of you would drink from this river, he is not going to continue with me, except if anyone would take just a mere sip with his hand." The majority of the army drank from the river.

Saul said, "You are not coming with me." A very small number did not drink.

Now, they crossed the river. The king and those who had faith, remember the word (faith), he and the faithful ones with him crossed the river. So those who crossed the rivers were believers. When they saw the army of Goliath, they said, "We cannot face Goliath and his army." Now these people were believers who did not drink from the river or only had a sip. But when they saw the might of Goliath, how many aircraft carriers he had there, how many rocket launchers, how many F16, F23, F30, whatever, when they saw the arsenal of Goliath, they said, "No way, we have no way to face Goliath and his army." But those who had faith that they are going to meet God, those who were convinced that they must meet God, "How often by God's will has a small force vanquished a big one. God is with those who steadfastly persevere."

Those were the children of Israel at the time of Prophet Samuel, at the time of King Saul. And what happened when now they are facing, physically facing advancing to meet Goliath and his force, you can see now what is left: a very, very, very small number are left to fight with Saul. What was the prayer they said, which the Palestinians are praying all the time, "Our Lord, pour out constancy on us and make our steps firm. Help us against those that reject the faith." They defeated them by the will of God, and David killed Goliath. God gave him power and wisdom and taught him whatever else he wished.

And then God ends this Verse, 251 in Chapter 2, by saying, **"Did not God check one set of people by means** *of another, the Earth would indeed be full of mischief. But God is full of bounty to all the worlds."*

Let me read the footnote before I stop. "Even in the small band that remained faithful, there were some who were appalled by the number of the enemy when they met him face to face and saw the size and strength of the enemy commander, the giant Goliath, Jalut. But there was a very small band who were determined to face all odds because they had perfect confidence in God and in the cause for which they were fighting. They were for making a firm stand and seeking God's help. Of that number was David. David was a raw youth with no arms or armour. He was not known even in the Israelite camp, and the giant Goliath mocked him. Even David's own elder brother chided him for deserting his sheep, for he was a poor shepherd lad to outward appearance. But his faith had made him more than a match for the Philistine hosts.

When Saul offered his own armour and arms to David, the young hero declined, as he had not tried them, while his shepherd sling and staff were his well-tried implements. He picked up five smooth pebbles on the spot from the stream and used his sling to such effect that he knocked down Goliath. He then used Goliath's own sword to slay him. There was consternation in the Philistine army; they broke and fled and were pursued and cut to pieces.

Apart from the main lesson that if we would preserve our national existence and our faith, it is our duty to fight with courage and firmness, there are other lessons in David's story.

1. *Numbers do not count but faith, determination, and the blessing of God.*
2. *Size and strength are of no avail against truth, courage, and careful planning.*
3. *The hero tries his own weapons and those that are available to him at the time and place, even though people may laugh at him.*
4. *If God is with us, the enemy's weapon may become an instrument of his own destruction.*
5. *Personality conquers all dangers and puts hearts into our own wavering friends.*
6. *Pure faith brings God's reward, which may take many forms.*

In David's case, it was power, wisdom, and other gifts which God gave him."

Thank you very much indeed for listening. God bless you all."

What the NSS said about my Friday Sermon:

"Qur'ani Murkuz Trust, which funds the South Woodford Islamic Centre in London. A video published on the centre's YouTube account says God's wrath 'will soon visit the oppressors and their supporters'. He says the 'current oppressors' are 'the 27 EU countries and Israel and the USA'. The lecturer continues: 'Unfortunately we live in a secular world where the majority of the people don't believe in God'. He says: 'Those who have faith fight in the way of God, while those who disbelieve fight in the way of Satan. Fight then against the friends of Satan.'

Our response to the NSS

Date: Mon, Dec 11, 2023 at 10:45 AM

"Dear National Secular Society,
We note that on 29 November 2023 you posted on your
website an article titled 'NSS refers 40+ Islamic charities to
regulator over extremism fear (your Article) which includes
a wholly misleading reference to us:
https://www.secularism.org.uk/news/2023/11/nss-refers-
40-islamic-charities-to-regulator-over-extremism-fears
It is very disappointing that before publishing your Article
you did not follow good practice and contact us to get our
response.

If you had, we would have advised you that South
Woodford Islamic Centre ("SWIC") serves a diverse
multicultural local community and adheres to applicable
laws and good practice. As such, we were very
disappointed to read your claim that SWIC has been
reported to the Charity Commission. As a reputable charity
we take all such claims and complaints seriously.

Having reviewed the video you mention in your Article, it is
patently clear that the NSS has selected (for reasons best
known to you) various quotes and has, for example, taken
them out of context and sensationalised them without
understanding that they were based on Qur'anic text etc.,
and did NOT promote extremism etc. Accordingly, we
respectfully reject and deny any and all allegations
purported to be made against us in the Article and will
vigorously defend ourselves, if necessary.

FYI, please note that on 13 October 2023 we issued a
public statement that we oppose the killing of non-

combatant civilians in Israel and other conflicts around the world irrespective of their religion or ethnicity or race and that foreign policy can only be changed by lobbying MPs and through peaceful and lawful demonstrations and petitions and not through any form of violence as this is against the teachings of Islam and also against the law.

If we receive any communication from the Charity Commission we will be happy to cooperate and work with them and respond accordingly.

In the light of the above we require that within 5 calendar days of this email you remove all references of Qur'ani Murkuz trust and South Woodford Islamic Centre from your Article and post a clarification on your website (as prominent as your Article and for such period as necessary) substantially in the form attached.

We assume that as a responsible organisation you will do this. For the avoidance of any doubt, we reserve our rights and no delay in exercising or non-exercise by us of any right, power or remedy provided by law or otherwise shall impair, or otherwise operate as a waiver or release of, that right, power or remedy.

Yours sincerely,
Trustees
Qur'ani Murkuz Trust"

Ironically, I'm very surprised that people who are secular and don't believe in God, are so worried about God's wrath befalling them!

We also received an email from the Political Editor of the Sunday Telegraph

30th November 2023

"Hi

I note that the Qur'ani Murkuz Trust has been reported to the Charity Commission as one of a series of charities propagating anti-Semitism, extremism and incitement to violence.

This is specifically in relation to a sermon given last month at the South Woodford Islamic Centre in London, which we note you manage and operate.

A video uploaded to YouTube shows the speaker stating that God's wrath 'will soon visit the oppressors and their supporters.' He says the 'current oppressors' are 'the 27 EU countries and Israel and the USA.'.
He continues: "Unfortunately we live in a secular world where the majority of the people don't believe in God."
He says: "Those who have faith fight in the way of God, while those who disbelieve fight in the way of Satan. Fight then against the friends of Satan."

Do you have any response to the allegation that your charity has been propagating anti-Semitism, extremism and incitement to violence by hosting the above sermon?

I would be grateful for a response by midday tomorrow (Friday).

Yours sincerely,

Edward Malnick
Political Editor, The Sunday Telegraph"

Our response to Mr Edward Malnick

"Dear Mr Malnick,

Thank you for your email of 30 November 2023.

Please note that South Woodford Islamic Centre (SWIC) is a professionally run place of worship which serves a diverse multicultural local community and adheres to applicable laws and good practice. As such, we were very disappointed to read your claim that SWIC has been reported to the Charity Commission. As a reputable charity we take all such claims and complaints seriously.

It appears that you are quoting from the National Secular Society ("NSS") website post of 29 November 2023 (https://www.secularism.org.uk/news/2023/11/nss-refers-40-islamic-charities-to- regulator-over-extremism-fears).

Having reviewed the video the NSS mention, which is of a sermon given on 13th October 2023, it is clear that the NSS has selected various quotes and have, for example, taken them out of context for reasons best known to them. Accordingly, we respectfully reject and deny any and all allegations purported to be made against us and will vigorously defend ourselves, if necessary.

FYI, please note that on 13 October 2023 we issued a public statement that we oppose the killing of noncombatant civilians in Israel and other conflicts around the world irrespective of their religion or ethnicity or race and that foreign policy can only be changed by lobbying MPs and through peaceful and lawful demonstrations and petitions and not through any form of violence as this is against the teachings of Islam and also against the law.

If we receive any communication from the Charity Commission we will be happy to cooperate and work with them and respond accordingly.

Yours sincerely,

Trustees

South Woodford Islamic Centre"

In response to the complaint made by NSS to the Charity Commission, we received a communication from the Charity Commission dated 11th December 2023, asking us to respond to the false allegations made by the NSS. Being a very highly respected and professionally run charity, we responded on 13th December 2023, in great detail to the Charity Commission and provided all the information they requested.

On 22nd November 2024, we received the final response from the Charity Commission, where they confirmed the following:

"The Commission has assessed the information made available in line with our published Regulatory and Risk

Framework1, including the information provided by the trustees. Based on this, the Commission has concluded that no further regulatory action is required at this time. We will therefore be closing our case into the Charity with the issuing of regulatory advice and guidance under section 15(2) of the Charities Act 20112 ('the Act') for the trustees to read, consider and act upon where appropriate."

The following recommendations were made by the Charity Commission. It is highly advisable that the trustees of every registered UK Muslim charity, must fully comply with these regulations.

1. The trustees must be made aware that any statements made by the Charity must fall in line with charity law and trustee's legal obligations and failure to do so may reflect negatively on the Charity and impact on its reputation and standing.
2. Care must be taken when speakers use words or phrases which are open to misinterpretation and/or may have multiple meanings. This can include, but is not limited to, quoting from scripture. This is particularly important where words or phrases could potentially be misinterpreted as calling for, condoning or supporting acts of violence.
3. The Commission acknowledges that freedom of expression is a key human right and the Commission does not seek to encroach on any individual's right to freedom of speech, expression or association and we recognise that recent events are emotive and distressing. That said, charity trustees must abide by charity law and other relevant laws generally. Trustees have a legal duty to protect the assets of their charity and this

includes its reputation. The careless or reckless use of language can have serious unintended consequences for a charity, and for the charity sector generally. This can include reputational damage to the Charity. Such actions can lead to the diversion of resources away from the Charity's core business in order to manage the consequences.

4. In addition, charities must operate for the public benefit and any harm they create must be overweight by their benefit to the public. In some instances, expressing partisan or strongly controversial views may compromise the charity's integrity or public trust and confidence in it. The responsibility for the management and control of a charity rests with the trustee and trustee should regularly review and assess the risks their charity faces. Where major risks are identified, the trustees will need to make sure that appropriate action is being taken to manage them.

5. The Trustee should ensure that they are familiar with the Commissions guidance Compliance Toolkit - Chapter 5: Protecting charities from abuse for extremist purposes. Whilst this guidance is written in a slightly different context, this guidance is particularly useful where Charities are looking to further their charity's objects through holding events, hosting speakers and making statements or engaging in debate on sensitive issues.

6. The Commission's guidance Charities and risk management (CC26) also provides guidance regarding trustees responsibilities with regards to regularly reviewing and assessing the risks faced

by the charity in all areas of its work and planning for the management of those risks.

7. With regards to the trustee's review of the Charity Speakers Policy, the trustees should refer to the guidance included within the Compliance Toolkit - Chapter 5: Protecting charities from abuse for extremist purposes - Section 10: Charity Events and Speakers, including taking account of Section 10.3 which states examples of the steps that you and your co-trustees can take to help you to manage the risks involved in hosting events and speakers at the Charity.

8. Trustees must ensure their charity is not undertaking political campaigning or activity if it is not in line with their charitable objects. Moving forwards, the trustees should ensure that they are familiar with the Commission's guidance; Campaigning and political activity guidance for charities - GOV.UK which sets out what charities need to consider when campaigning or engaging in political activity. The trustees should also consider whether this guidance also needs to be made available to any employees, volunteers or speakers at the Charity who are active on social media and can easily be linked to the Charity.

9. Additionally, the trustees should refer to the following Commission guidance;
   - The essential trustee: what you need to know, what you need to do (CC3)
   - Charities and social media

As you can see from the above, the culture of free speech of which I was so enamoured when I first migrated to the UK in 1970, is simply a beautiful dream.

Stifling debate is not a way forward in this crisis

I recall that I received a hostile response to a speech I gave at Holocaust Memorial Day in the London Borough of Redbridge, on 27th January 2009. At the time of writing my speech, there was a war going on in Gaza. I strongly felt thatI had to refer to it in my speech, if I were to address injustice in the world. I forwarded the draft of my speech to a Jewish friend of mine, College Director, to check whether I had made any inappropriate comments which would not be suitable for the occasion. He was so happy with what I had written.

Below is the speech I delivered that day. The theme was "Stand up to Hatred":

"Dear brothers and sisters. May God's Peace, Mercy and Blessings be upon all of you.

I am honoured to participate in Holocaust Memorial Day. According to the Oxford Dictionary hatred means active dislike, enmity or ill-will. Hatred might be due to jealousy, injustice, ignorance, arrogance or greed.

Let me give you a few examples. Before the creation of Adam, God commanded the Angels and the Spirit to prostrate themselves to Adam once he was created. They all obeyed, except Satan. When God asked him, 'Why did you not prostrate yourself to Adam when I commanded you?' Satan replied: 'I'm better than him. You created me from fire and him from Clay.' That was the first ever racist remark. He arrogantly despised the angels who prostrated as well as the man to whom they prostrated to and he was in rebellion against God for not obeying His order. Arrogance, jealousy and rebellion were his triple crime. Thus, racism in any form is a crime against God.

We are all brothers and sisters in humanity. God says in 49:13: "Oh mankind! We created you from a single (pair) of a male and a female, and made you into nations and tribes, that you may know each (not that you may despise each other). Verily the most honoured of you in the sight of God is (he who is) the most righteous of you. And God has full knowledge and is well acquainted (with all things)"

Unfortunately, animosity can lead to hate crimes. The first hate crime committed was by Cain, the son of Adam, who was puffed up with arrogance and jealousy, which led him to murder his righteous and innocent brother Abel.

Another hate crime was committed when the children of Jacob decided out of jealousy to throw their brother Joseph in the well to get rid of him. Jacob stood up to hatred and embarked on a rehabilitation programme to save his children from the wrath of God. Eventually their repugnance to Joseph turned into true love. The Prophet Mohammed said: 'Hate your enemy mildly, he may become your friend one day.' (Al-Tirmidhi)
I'm a preacher, not a politician. It is against my faith to incite hatred or sow enmity between people. I have a code of conduct to follow. God says in 16:125: "Invite (all) to the way of your Lord with wisdom and beautiful preaching; and argue with them in ways that are best and most gracious: for your Lord knows best who have strayed from His Path, and who receive guidance."

Unfortunately, there are politicians who would incite hatred to win an election and the political system does not check them. For example, my ward councillor comes from a party which invents lies against the ethnic minorities to win elections. Almost 30 years ago my house in Woodford and my cars were attacked on daily basis forcing me to move out of the area. Ten years ago, our mosque at South Woodford was burnt down. Hate crimes continue against the Muslim community and their buildings in the UK.

Last October I visited the Holy Land with 22 Muslims, two Christians and Rabbi David Hulbert all from the Three Faiths Forum in East London on a mission of peace and reconciliation. While there we visited the Holocaust Memorial Yad Vashem in Jerusalem. It was a moving experience to see the level of atrocities committed against innocent civilians. I said to our Israeli guide: 'shame on those who deny the Holocaust. It is not the number; it is the principle.

God says in 5:32: 'On that account: We ordained for the Children of Israel that if anyone slew a person -unless it be for murder or for spreading mischief in the land -it would be as if he slew the whole people. And if anyone saved a life, it would be as if he saved the life of the whole people'

A similar verse is also in the Talmud. The Israeli guide hugged me while crying saying: 'God bless you Mohammed.' Unfortunately, in the last few weeks the world witnessed atrocities committed against innocent civilians in Gaza while the Israeli army was launching a disproportionate war against Hamas to silence their rockets of terror.

Many Jews worldwide and in the UK condemned the killing of civilians. The article written by Avi Shlaim, Professor of International Relations at Oxford University, published in the Guardian on Wednesday 7th January 2009, and the one written by Uri Avenry 'How many Divisions?' published by Gush Shalom demonstrate that there are many intellectual Jews who support and stand firm for peace and justice.

God confirms the great qualities of such people in verse 7:159: 'Of the people of Moses there is a section who guide and do justice in the light of truth.'

The Holocaust of the 2nd World War has not been the last of its kind. So, the question is, why couldn't we learn from history? Why can't we see the parallels in history? Why do we continue to hate and translate this hate into harm for other people? At each stage, positions become more entrenched and communities around the world begin to take on a role not much different from football supporters who support their team right or wrong.

God says in verse 4:135: 'Oh you who believe! Stand out firmly for justice as witnesses to God, even as against yourselves, or your parents, or your kin, and whether it be (against) rich or poor. For God can best protect both. Don't follow the lusts (of your hearts), lest you swerve, and if you distort (justice) or decline to do justice, verily God is well acquainted with all that you do.'
And He says in verse 5:8: 'Oh you who believe! Stand firmly for God, as witnesses to fair dealing, and don't let the hatred of others to you make you swerve to wrong and depart from justice. Be just, that is next to Piety, and fear God. For God is well-acquainted with all that you do.'

Disagreeing with a government's policy does not mean you become anti the people of that country. So let not the Middle East crisis affect the relationship between Muslims and Jews in Britain. Let us continue to respect and love each other and work together to achieve peace and harmony for our communities here and lasting peace in the Middle East. We must recognise the danger. If one group will fall, the other will follow."

Did I say anything wrong in the above speech? Did I incite hatred against anyone?

Surprisingly, the moment I mentioned Gaza, while delivering my speech, I could hear extremely aggressive comments thrown at me. Just after finishing, I was physically and verbally abused by some members of the Jewish community. One of them pulled the collar of my coat and shouted at me: "How dare you mention Gaza? You have no sensitivity". My throat became so dry, but I had to fully control myself as I didn't want to create a scene.

While walking out, I met two Councillors from Redbridge, a husband and wife who were my neighbours. They both greeted me nicely and said: "Well done for mentioning Gaza!" I was so disappointed that they did not have the courage to publicly denounce the killing of innocent people in Gaza. They were concerned about losing their seats in the next election.

On Friday 30th January, after delivering the Friday sermon at my mosque, I told the congregation what happened on the day. Two young men came to me and said: "We are from Afghanistan. Shall we sort them out?" I was shocked to hear that. I said: "I know you love me so much. But as good practicing British Muslims we should never resort to violence. It is against God's Moral Law." They thanked me and left peacefully.

Chris Grant, the Editor of the Ilford Recorder, wrote a very fair and supporting article on 29th January 2009, with the title "Stifling debate not way forward in this crisis".

Under a photo of mine with a rabbi, Mr Grant wrote: "BRAVE STATEMENT: Imam Mohammed Fahim speaking at the Holocaust Memorial Day service on Tuesday, in Valentines Park, Ilford."

Mr Grant said: "...The Gaza crisis featured heavily during the Holocaust Memorial Day service on Tuesday. Redbridge Council leader Cllr Alan Weinberg's stark message was that 'the world has learned nothing. We are killing each other for no reason.' In his speech representing the Muslim community, Imam Mohammed Fahim, spoke out against racism and hatred towards all people, but also told of 'atrocities committed against innocent civilians in Gaza' and accused the Israeli army of launching a 'disproportionate war against Hamas to silence their rockets of terror'. That statement was brave in the circumstances and was not well received by some of those gathered. But Redbridge must be strong enough to allow debate about such issue. Surely, many of the conflicts in this world are caused by people not having a voice or being unable to have any say in their future. That's why *measured debate must continue to be encouraged between the communities, in order that everyone's voice is heard."*

Mr H Harris, from Cranbrook Road, Gants Hill, wrote to the Editor of the Recorder, on 12th February 2009, attacking me:

"The Holocaust Memorial event at Valentines Park last week was well represented by all faiths and school children. Sadly, the Muslim cleric tarnished it by denouncing Israel's bombing of Gaza. No one is proud that innocent people of Gaza were killed, but Hamas has, over the past two years, fired rockets into Israel. Why is it acceptable to give a preacher a platform to incite racial hatred?"

The Guardian newspaper wrote in their issue dated 29th January 2009: *"...During a ceremony at the Holocaust memorial garden in Valentines Park, Ilford, speakers including Dr Mohammed Fahim, Imam of South Woodford Mosque, Rabbi Aryeh Sufrin from the Chabad Lubavitch Centre, and Council Leader Alan Weinberg, spoke about the importance of the day and of the need to fight prejudice and hate in today..."*

Redbridge official newspaper "Redbridge Life", wrote in February 2009, under 'Council and faith leaders unite to oppose religious hatred': *"Council leaders from the three main parties have united with Jewish and Muslim leaders to collectively oppose any form of violence or hatred carried out in the name of their religions. The political and faith leaders decided to issue a joint statement to make it clear they believe religious tensions around the world must not be allowed to affect good community relations in Redbridge."* I was so happy to be one of the signatories to the joint statement.

The Mayor of Redbridge, Cllr Mrs Loraine Sladden, wrote to me on 30th January 2009:

"Dear Dr Fahim,

Holocaust Memorial Day

I wanted to write to thank you very much for the contribution that you made to Holocaust Memorial Day on 27th January.

I believe that it is very important to the community in Redbridge that we continue to commemorate those who suffered and died in the Holocaust and I thank you for your support. The presence of yourself as a representative of the Muslim community helps send a very positive message about community cohesion in Redbridge and I appreciate it.

Yours sincerely

Councillor Mrs Loraine Sladden"

Was the Hamas attack Islamically justified?

On 8th November 2024, the BBC reported that the most prominent Islamic scholar in Gaza had issued a rare, powerful fatwa condemning Hamas' 7 October 2023 attack on Israel, which triggered the devastating war in the Palestinian territory. The BBC says, *"Professor Dr Salman al-Dayah, a former dean of the Faculty of Sharia and Law at the Hamas-affiliated Islamic University of Gaza, is one of the region's most respected religious authorities, so his legal opinion carries significant weight among Gaza's two million population, which is predominantly Sunni Muslim.*

"A fatwa is a non-binding Islamic legal ruling from a respected religious scholar usually based on the Qur'an or the Sunnah - the sayings and practices of the Prophet Muhammad. Dr Dayah's fatwa, which was published in a detailed six-page document, criticises Hamas for what he calls 'violating Islamic principles governing jihad'"

Dr Dayah adds: *"If the pillars, causes, or conditions of jihad are not met, it must be avoided in order to avoid destroying people's lives. This is something that is easy to guess for our country's politicians, so the attack must have been avoided."*

The above reported fatwa by the BBC, echoes the findings of my research published in my book **"Confused Muslims.Qom - Confessions of a London Imam"**. In Chapter One, *"We Can Defeat Terrorism Together"*, I discuss the different types of jihad and martyrdom in Islam, drawing from the Qur'an and the Prophetic Tradition of

Prophet Muhammad (pbuh). I feel as if Professor Dr Salman al-Dayah is saying: "*6th October 1973 attack by Egypt, was justifiable. But 7th October 2023 attack by Hamas was not justifiable. Hamas should have accepted the State of Israel and made peace with it, and Israel should have recognised Gaza as an independent demilitarised State and lived together side by side in peace*".

That was also my sweet dream which became a nightmare.

Chapter Twenty - What world leaders and human rights organisations are saying about the conflict

Prime ministers, presidents, and global leaders convened in New York City for the 79th session of the United Nations General Assembly on October 1, 2024.The ongoing conflict in Gaza emerged as the central focus of many of the speeches delivered during the session. Here are some key excerpts from these speeches:

UN Secretary-General Antonio Guterres

"The speed and scale of the killing and destruction in Gaza are unlike anything in my years as secretary-general. More than 200 of our own staff have been killed, many with their families. Gaza is a nonstop nightmare that threatens to take the entire region with it. The international community must mobilise for an immediate ceasefire, the immediate and unconditional release of all hostages, and the beginning of an irreversible process towards a two-state solution."

Brazilian President Luiz Inacio Lula da Silva

"In Gaza and the West Bank, we are witnessing one of the greatest humanitarian crises in recent history, now spreading dangerously to Lebanon.Israel's response in the

*wake of the Hamas attacks on October 7 has become a
collective punishment for the entire Palestinian people.
There are more than 40,000 fatal victims, most of them
women and children.The right to defence has become the
right to revenge, which prevents an agreement to release
hostages and postpones the ceasefire."*

US President Joe Biden

*"Innocent civilians in Gaza are also going through hell.
Thousands and thousands killed, including aid workers.
Too many families dislocated, crowding into tents, facing a
dire humanitarian situation.*

*As we look ahead we must also address the rise of
violence against innocent Palestinians on the West Bank
and set the conditions for a better future, including a two-
state solution where the world where Israel enjoys security
and peace and full recognition and normalised relations
with all its neighbours, where Palestinians live in security,
dignity, and self-determination in a state of their own.*

*I put forward with Qatar and Egypt a ceasefire and hostage
deal. It's been endorsed by the UN Security Council. Now
is the time for the parties to finalise its terms, bring the
hostages home, secure security for Israel, and Gaza free
of Hamas's grip, ease the suffering in Gaza, and end this
war."*

Turkish President Recep Tayyip Erdogan

"As a result of the Israeli attacks, Gaza has become the largest cemetery for children and women in the world: Over 17,000 children have been the targets of Israeli bullets and bombs.In Gaza, not only are children dying, but also the United Nations system. The values the West claims to defend are dying, the truth is dying, and the hopes of humanity to live in a more just world are dying – one by one.I am asking you bluntly here: Are those in Gaza and the occupied West Bank not human beings? Do children in Palestine have no rights?"

Jordan's King Abdullah II

"It often feels that there was not a moment when our world was not in turmoil. And yes, I cannot recall a time of greater peril than this. For nearly a year, the sky-blue flag flying over UN shelters and schools in Gaza has been powerless to protect innocent civilians from Israeli bombardment. So, it's no surprise that both inside and outside this hall, trust in the UN's cornerstone principles and ideals is crumbling.The harsh reality many see is that some nations are above international law, that global justice does bend to the will of power, and that human rights are selective; a privilege to be granted or denied at will."

Colombia President Gustavo Petro

"That richest 1 percent of humanity, the powerful global oligarchy, is the one that allows bombs to be dropped on the women, elderly, and children of Gaza, Lebanon, or Sudan. The power of a country in the world is no longer exercised by the type of economic or political system it has or its ideology but power is wielded according to how much capacity one has to destroy humankind. That is why we are not listened to when we vote to stop the genocide in Gaza. Even though we are the majority of the presidents of the world and represent the majority of humanity, we are not listened to by a minority of presidents who can stop the bombing."

Emir of Qatar Sheikh Tamim bin Hamad Al Thani

"Every year I stand on this podium and begin my speech by talking about the Palestinian cause, the absence of justice, the perils of believing that it can be neglected, and the illusions of making peace without a just solution. The ongoing Israeli aggression for nearly a year is nothing but a result of the absence of a sincere political will, deliberate international failure to resolve the Palestinian issue with a just solution, and insistence of the occupying Israeli authorities to impose a fait accompli on the Palestinians and the world with all types of force....

There is no Israeli partner for peace during the current government's tenure, and no peace process taking place, but rather a genocide. The end of the occupation and the Palestinian people exercising their right to self-determination is neither a favour nor a gift from anyone.

Unfortunately, the Security Council has failed to implement its ceasefire resolution in the Gaza Strip and to refrain from granting the state of Palestine full membership status in the United Nations despite the General Assembly's adoption of a resolution supporting Palestine's request for UN membership last May."

South African President Cyril Ramaphosa

"The violence the Palestinian people are being subjected to is a grim continuation of more than half a century of apartheid.We South Africans know what apartheid looks like. We lived through it. We suffered and died under it. We will not remain silent and watch as apartheid is perpetrated against others.In December last year, South Africa approached the International Court of Justice seeking an order to prevent Israel from committing genocide against the people of Gaza."

Iranian President Masoud Pezeshkian

"Over the past year, the world has witnessed the true nature of the Israeli regime. It has witnessed how this regime carries out atrocities in Gaza; and in eleven months has murdered in cold blood over 41,000 innocent people— mostly women and children.

Its leaders label this genocide; the killing of children, war crimes, and state terrorism as "legitimate self-defence".They label the freedom-loving and brave people around the world who protest against their genocide as "anti-Semitic".

They label an oppressed people, who have stood up against seven decades of occupation and humiliation, as "terrorists".

Belgium Prime Minister Alexander De Croo

"In the Middle East, decades of dehumanising the enemy has led to a vicious cycle of violence, resulting in the killing of over 40,000 people in less than a year. Early on in the Gaza war, my government warned against lack of respect for international humanitarian laws on both sides, and the disproportionate attack with blatant disregard for Palestinian civilian life.

We've been calling for an immediate and lasting ceasefire for many months, but today it seems more distant than ever. Hostilities need to stop before the whole region becomes engulfed in violence.Action speaks louder than words. Belgium has imposed a weapons embargo. We never ceased our support to UNRWA and other humanitarian organisations."

French President Emmanuel Macron

"Israel's war in Gaza has gone on for too long. The tens of thousands of Palestinian civilian casualties cannot be justified or explained away. Too many innocent people have died and we mourn them, as well.

This war must, therefore, end and a ceasefire must be achieved as quickly as possible, along with the release of the hostages and a massive flow of humanitarian aid into Gaza.

It is absolutely crucial for a new phase to begin in Gaza, for the weapons to fall silent, for humanitarian workers to return, and for civilian populations to be protected."

UK Prime Minister Keir Starmer

"Around the world, more fires are breaking out and burning with ever greater intensity. Exacting a terrible toll in Gaza, Lebanon, Ukraine, Sudan, Myanmar, Yemen, and beyond. I call on Israel and Hezbollah: Stop the violence. Step back from the brink. We need to see an immediate ceasefire to provide space for a diplomatic settlement, and we are working with all partners to that end. Because further escalation serves no one. This is intimately linked with the situation in Gaza where, again, we need to see an immediate ceasefire. It shames us all that the suffering in Gaza continues to grow."

Pakistan Prime Minister Shehbaz Sharif

"Can we, as human beings, remain silent while children lie buried, under the rubble of their shattered homes?
Can we turn a blind eye to the mothers, cradling the lifeless bodies of their children?
This is not just a conflict; this is systematic slaughter of innocent people; an assault on the very essence of human life and dignity. The blood of Gaza's children stains the

hands of not just the oppressors,☐ but☐ also of those who are complicit in prolonging this cruel conflict."

Barbados Prime Minister Mia Mottley

"And let me be clear, we condemn the actions of Hamas on October 7, but we equally and strongly deplore the humanitarian catastrophe in Gaza, which is the result of the disproportionate use of force by Israel.There's no justification for it and that is why treaties exist governing the rules of engagement for war."

Chinese Foreign Minister Wang Yi

"The question of Palestine is the biggest wound to human conscience. As we speak, the conflict in Gaza is still going on, causing more civilian casualties with each passing day. Fighting has spread to Lebanon; might must not take the place of justice.Palestine's long-held aspiration to establish an independent state should not be shunned any more, and the historical injustice suffered by the Palestinian people should not be ignored any longer.There must not be any delay in reaching a comprehensive ceasefire, and the fundamental way out lies in the two-state solution."

Russian Foreign Minister Sergey Lavrov

"All those who are still capable of compassion resent the fact that the October tragedy is being used for a massive collective punishment of the Palestinians, which has turned out to be an unprecedented humanitarian disaster.The

murder of Palestinian civilians by US weapons must stop.The delivery of humanitarian cargoes to the enclave must be ensured, the restoration of infrastructure must be arranged and, most importantly, the implementation of the legitimate right of self-determination of the Palestinians must be guaranteed, and they must be allowed to establish a territorially integral and viable state within the borders of 1967 with its capital in East Jerusalem, not in words but in deeds, "on the ground".

Indonesia Minister for Foreign Affairs Retno Lestari Priansari Marsudi

"Prime Minister Benjamin Netanyahu yesterday mentioned, and I quote, that "Israel seeks peace," that "Israel yearns for peace". Really? How are we supposed to believe that statement?Yesterday, while he was here, Israel conducted unprecedented massive air attacks on Beirut. PM Netanyahu wants the war to continue … We must stop that.We must pressure Israel to come back to a political solution for the two-state solution.As I speak now more than 41,000 in Gaza have been killed, the situation in West Bank Lebanon is deteriorating.Is that not enough? Will the Security Council only take action to stop Israel's atrocities when all Palestinian are displaced? Or when 100,000 Palestinians are killed? Or when a regional armed conflict breaks out? That will be too late!"

Malaysia Minister for Foreign Affairs Mohamad Hasan

"Just months ago, the world witnessed Israel's mockery, and utter disrespect of the United Nations in this very hall, with the insolent shredding of the UN Charter.Israel's actions, with each passing day, raise our doubts as to whether it actually believes in the UN system, or values its membership in this organisation.Let there be no doubt: The question of Gaza is a direct test of the capability of the United Nations. Let this 76-year-old issue not age into a century of our failure to uphold justice. Let our dreams of a free Palestine live beyond today, and beyond the words that we say."

Spanish Prime Minister Pedro Sanchez

"In Palestine, for almost a year now we've been witnessing an unconscionable spiral of death and devastation which is now, unfortunately, spreading to Lebanon.This is an escalation of the conflict, which is woefully grave in nature.

Spain condemns in the strongest terms the death of innocent civilians once again and consequently, I wish to once again call for de-escalation, detente and diplomacy.

We must put an end to the conflict in Gaza and tackle the root causes of the Israeli-Palestinian conflict, that's the only way that we'll be able to successfully extinguish the hotbeds of tension that are jeopardising regional and global stability.

Everything we're seeing daily in Gaza, and now unfortunately in Lebanon, is forcing us to think about the very validity of international humanitarian law just as we mark the 75th anniversary of the Geneva Conventions."

Palestinian President Mahmoud Abbas

"The massacres, the crimes, the genocide that Israel has been perpetrating against our people since its inception in 1948 to this very day will not go unpunished; there is no statute of limitations. But despite repeated calls, the world has not succeeded in obliging Israel to stop this war of genocide and its war crimes against innocent civilians.Palestinian people, for almost a year now, have been "subjected to one of the most heinous crimes of our era".Seventy-five percent of everything in Gaza has been fully destroyed.The world bears responsibility for the situation of our people in Gaza and the West Bank.We want a solution that will protect both countries, the State of Palestine and the State of Israel, so that they can coexist in peace, stability and security."

Israeli Prime Minister Benjamin Netanyahu

"To speak for my country, to speak for the truth. And here's the truth: Israel seeks peace. Israel yearns for peace. Israel has made peace and will make peace again.

Yet we face savage enemies who seek our annihilation, and we must defend ourselves against them.

In measured military operations, we destroyed nearly all of Hamas's terror battalions – 23 out of 24 battalions. Now, to complete our victory, we are focused on mopping up Hamas's remaining fighting capabilities.

Israel must also defeat Hezbollah in Lebanon."

As you can see from the above speeches, the majority of world leaders were concerned about the humanitarian crisis in Gaza and they were calling for an end to the violence and the suffering of the innocent civilians in Palestine and the return of the Israeli hostages.

I now give below the comments made by His Holiness Pope Francis on Monday 25th November 2024, as reported by the Middle East Monitor:

"Pope Francis condemned on Monday what he called the "arrogance of occupiers" in Ukraine and Palestine in a rare stance against Israeli policy and a week after he first addressed the allegations of genocide levelled against Israel. Speaking at the Vatican on the 40th anniversary of the peace treaty between Chile and Argentina, the Roman Catholic pontiff spoke of 'current armed conflicts' and the 'very painful suffering' they cause.

'I simply recall two failures of humanity today; in Ukraine and Palestine, where suffering is great and the arrogance of the occupier undermines dialogue,' he told diplomats and religious representatives in an improvised statement. He again criticised the arms trade, referring to the 'hypocrisy of talking about peace while waging war.' Dialogue, added the pontiff, must be the essence of the international community.

The Pope regularly offers prayers for the civilians in Gaza and Ukraine 'who are suffering greatly' as well as for the release of the Israeli captives held by Hamas since the movement's unprecedented cross-border incursion on 7 October, 2023. He received 16 former Israeli hostages on 14 November at the Vatican.

Last week, Pope Francis suggested that the global community should study whether Israel's military campaign in Gaza constituted genocide of the Palestinian people, in some of his most explicit criticism yet of Israel's conduct in its year-long war.

In a new book, Hope Never Disappoints. Pilgrims Towards a Better World, the leader of the world's 1.4 billion Roman Catholics said, 'According to some experts, what is happening in Gaza has the characteristics of genocide.' Extracts were published on Sunday in Italy's La Stampa. The book is scheduled to be published next Tuesday.

'Israel's attacks in Gaza and Lebanon are immoral and disproportionate,' said the Pope in September, adding that the Israeli army had exceeded the rules of war.

This is the first time the head of the Roman Catholic Church has publicly condemned Israeli policy in the occupied Palestinian Territory in such terms."

Al Jazeera reported on 25th December 2024, the Christmas message given by His Holiness Pope Francis:

"In his Christmas addresses on 25th December 2024, Pope Francis has denounced the 'extremely grave' humanitarian situation in Gaza while appealing for the release of captives and a ceasefire in the war-torn coastal enclave.

In his Christmas 'Urbi et Orbi' (to the city and world) address on Wednesday at the Vatican, Francis also appealed for peace in Ukraine and Sudan.

'I think of the Christian communities in Israel and Palestine, particularly in Gaza, where the humanitarian situation is extremely grave. May there be a ceasefire, may the hostages be released and aid be given to the people worn out by hunger and by war.' he said.

The 88-year-old, celebrating the 12th Christmas of his pontificate, called for an end to conflicts, political, social or military, in places including Lebanon, Mali, Mozambique, Haiti, Venezuela and Nicaragua.

'I invite every individual, and all people of all nations … to become pilgrims of hope, to silence the sounds of arms and overcome divisions,' the pope said."

I give below an abstract from the article written by Al Jazeera columnist, Andrew Metrovica, on 31st December 2024:

"Like you and me, the Pope can see what Israel has done with such ruthless ferocity to besieged Palestinians for more than a year in the barren, dystopian remnants of Gaza and the occupied West Bank.

I believe that Francis understands that bearing witness to human suffering and misery on an almost incomprehensible scale requires a response, that silence under the awful, prevailing circumstances means, at the least, blithe acceptance and, at the worst, conscious complicity.

So, to his credit, the Pontiff has said what needed to be said. The Pope has, in effect, abandoned neutrality in favour of a raw, refreshing honesty to declare - with candid language - his sympathy for and solidarity with the millions of Palestinian victims of Israel's relentless killing lust.

I am convinced that Francis will be remembered for having taken an honourable stand at the right time for the right reasons while so many other "leaders" in Europe and beyond have armed an apartheid regime with the weapons and diplomatic cover to engineer a still unfolding 21st century genocide.

Francis will be remembered, as well, for rebuffing efforts to intimidate or bully him to qualify or retract statements made from 'the heart' that Israel is guilty of 'cruelty' as it goes methodically about reducing much of Gaza and the West Bank to dust and memory. Instead, bolstered by the truth and an apt sense of righteousness, the Pontiff has refused to step back or 'soften' his remarks.

The Pope's defiance is not only admirable but also tangible evidence that he does not intend to forsake Palestinians."

Report by Human Rights Watch:

BBC reported on 15 Nov 24 that Israel has committed war crimes and crimes against humanity by deliberately causing the mass displacement of Palestinians in Gaza, a report by Human Rights Watch (HRW) says.

About 1.9 million people - 90% of Gaza's population - have fled their homes over the past year, and 79% of the territory is under Israeli-issued evacuation orders, according to the UN.

HRW's report says this amounts to "forcible transfer" and that "evidence shows it has been systematic and part of a state policy". It also says Israeli actions appear to "meet the definition of ethnic cleansing".

Israel said the report was "completely false and detached from reality".

HRW has also accused Hamas of using civilians as human shields by operating inside homes and civilian infrastructure.

Report by Amnesty International:

Al Jazeera reported that human rights group Amnesty International has concluded that Israel's war on Gaza meets the legal threshold for genocide in a damning new report.

The report published on Thursday, 5th December 2024, titled, "You Feel Like You Are Subhuman": Israel's Genocide Against Palestinians in Gaza, is the culmination of months of research by Amnesty, including extensive witness interviews, analysis of "visual and digital evidence", including satellite imagery, and statements made by senior Israeli government and military officials.

Amnesty said the Israeli military has committed at least three of the five acts banned by the 1948 Genocide Convention, including indiscriminate killings of civilians, causing serious bodily or mental harm, and "deliberately inflicting on Palestinians in Gaza conditions of life calculated to bring about their physical destruction".

"Month after month, Israel has treated Palestinians in Gaza as a subhuman group unworthy of human rights and dignity, demonstrating its intent to physically destroy them," said Agnes Callamard, secretary-general of Amnesty International.

"Our research reveals that, for months, Israel has persisted in committing genocidal acts, fully aware of the irreparable harm it was inflicting on Palestinians in Gaza," Callamard said.

"It continued to do so in defiance of countless warnings about the catastrophic humanitarian situation and of legally binding decisions from the International Court of Justice [ICJ] ordering Israel to take immediate measures to enable the provision of humanitarian assistance to civilians in Gaza," she said.

"Our damning findings must serve as a wake-up call to the international community: this is genocide. It must stop now," she added.

Callamard said that taking into "account the pre-existing context of dispossession, apartheid and unlawful military occupation" in which the Israeli military's crimes against the civilian population of Gaza have been committed, "we could find only one reasonable conclusion: Israel's intent is the physical destruction of Palestinians in Gaza".

Israel dismissed the Amnesty International report as "entirely false" on Thursday.

"The deplorable and fanatical organisation Amnesty International has once again produced a fabricated report that is entirely false and based on lies," Israel's foreign ministry said in a statement

How did the BBC respond to the Report by Amnesty International?

BBC reported on 5th December 2024, that Amnesty International has accused Israel of committing genocide against Palestinians in the Gaza war, which Israel strongly denies.

The UK-based human rights group said its conclusion was based on "dehumanising and genocidal statements" by Israeli officials, digital images and witness testimony and must serve as "a wake-up call" to the international community.

Israel's foreign ministry described the 295-page report as "entirely false and based on lies", while the Israeli military said the claims were "entirely baseless and fail to account for the operational realities" it faces.

The response of Muslim Council of Britain to Amnesty's report:

"Amnesty International Published Damning Report on Genocide in Gaza, on December 6, 2024.

The Muslim Council of Britain (MCB) expresses grave concern following the publication of Amnesty International's damning report of genocide in Gaza. The report highlights that the government of Israel has subjected Palestinians in Gaza to continuous and deliberate harm, treating them as a subhuman group unworthy of basic human rights and dignity. Amnesty International underscores that these actions demonstrate a specific intent to physically destroy Palestinians in Gaza, meeting the legal definition of genocide.

This alarming report comes as Gaza continues to face relentless bombardment, with civilians enduring unprecedented suffering and destruction.

The UN Secretary-General has warned that the humanitarian catastrophe unfolding in Gaza demands urgent international action to protect civilians and prevent further escalation.

The MCB calls on the UK government to heed the warnings issued by Amnesty International and the International Court of Justice (ICJ). Immediate steps must be taken to ensure accountability, prevent further atrocities, and work towards a permanent ceasefire to end the suffering in Gaza."

A testimony from an Israeli Historian:

An Israeli historian's testimony of the horrible situation in the Gaza Strip
Bearing Witness to the Israel-Gaza War (March 17th 2024)
- LEE MORDECHAI

"I, Lee Mordechai, a historian and an Israeli citizen, testify in this document, as events are unfolding, to the horrible situation in the Gaza Strip. I write my personal opinion out of a sense of double responsibility: as a citizen whose country is committing what I consider as grave crimes, and as an academic, who believes that after having dedicated my career to research I am obliged to speak up against injustice, especially when it is so close. I write also because of the disappointing general silence on this issue among many international and Israeli academic institutions, especially those that are well-positioned to comment on it. The relatively few of my colleagues who have bravely spoken out have been an inspiration. I do not believe this document will convince many others to change

their minds. Rather, I write this publicly to testify that during the war there were and remain Israeli voices who strongly dissented from Israel's actions.

"The newest version of this document can be found on my academia.edu and Twitter pages, which also have an English version. Older versions appear on my Twitter page. I plan to continue to revise this document every few weeks. I include in this document a large number of references, especially of videos from Gaza, to convey and clarify the scale of this event and the frequency of the horrors that I describe."

What did the British Palestinian Committee (BPC) say?

On Tuesday 28th January 2025, Al Jazeera published the following report: "The United Kingdom's military collaboration with Israel during its assault on Gaza, as well as its support through arms provisions, logistical aid, and direct military interventions in Yemen to support Israel's objectives, could constitute a breach of international law, a new report reveals.

The report, released on Tuesday 28th January 2025, by the British Palestinian Committee (BPC), says while the UK government has not been directly perpetrating violence in Gaza, it has 'played an influential role' through the validation of arms licences and wider, deeper military collaboration with Israel.

'UK ministers and officials know that the UK has obligations under international law,' Sara Husseini, BPC director, told Al Jazeera.

'They have recognised that Israel's illegal occupation is ongoing and they have been made aware by the world's highest court that Israel's actions in Gaza plausibly amount to genocide.

'We are, therefore, calling on the government to immediately impose a two-way arms embargo, end all forms of military collaboration, and uphold the inalienable rights of the Palestinian people. If not, the British government should face appropriate legal consequences.'

In the 19-page report, the BPC concluded that the UK is legally obligated to take measures to prevent genocide and to prosecute individuals or entities responsible for committing such acts, both within its own jurisdiction and, where feasible, internationally.

The group also stressed that the obligation of states to prevent genocide is a proactive rather than a passive action and entails the concept of 'due diligence', necessitating an assessment based on factual evidence.

In 2022, the UK supplied 42 million pounds ($53m) worth of arms to Israel, according to media reports."

Chapter Twenty One - Conclusion

The stories in the Qur'an show historic moral examples of the downfall of tyrants and call on God's servants to remain patient in times of oppression and have faith in His ultimate judgment and will.

Qarun's downfall came after he dismissed the warnings of his people, believing that his wealth made him invincible and that his success was solely due to his own abilities. Similarly, all humans can face the same fate if they follow the path of arrogance.

God has taught us that it is the righteous, not the wealthy, who attain success in this life and the Hereafter. Wealth or power without righteousness leads to ruin and downfall, as history has shown time and time again.

This offers a glimpse of hope to the Palestinian people, who are currently enduring severe oppression, showing that all is not lost.

The history told in the Qur'an emphasises the importance of steadfastness in faith, even when immediate results are not visible. If we cannot see the light at the end of the tunnel for Palestinians, it is because our foresight is merely human. God knows what we do not, God sees what we do not and God plans what we can not.

The story of Prophet Jacob and his sons serve as an inspiration for humanity, where we can see parallels between the suffering of the Israelites under Pharaoh and the modern-day oppression of the Palestinians. I remember this story every time I stand next to my Jewish brothers and sisters who stand in solidarity with Palestinians. We come together through our shared values of justice and empathy for the oppressed. From such blessed interactions and studying of the sacred texts, it is clear that what we are seeing in Gaza has no scriptural basis, or justification in any of God's texts.

Speaking out against human rights violations, regardless of the identity of the perpetrator, is not an act of Anti-Semitism but rather a moral imperative that aligns with the principles of justice and compassion.

From the Balfour declaration to the horrific crimes against humanity during the Holocaust, it is important to recognise that Anti-Semitism, particularly in Christian Europe, has manifested in various harmful forms throughout history, and these distinctions must not be conflated with legitimate calls for justice in the defence of those who are being oppressed in Palestine.

History has provided us with lessons, the international community has provided us with standards and demands; but above all, God has provided us with His promise. Humanity will prevail and those who stand for justice, regardless of their gender, race, faith or creed, will be victorious.

As it was then, so it is now. In spite of the obvious Signs of God, people who are blind in their obstinance to Truth accomplish their own destruction, while humble, persecuted men of Faith are transformed by the Light of God and obtain salvation. Nothing that the powers of evil can do will ever defeat the merciful Purpose of God. Evil, in resisting good, will affect its own destruction.

God warns the unbelievers in Verse 9:32, that they will never be able to extinguish His light:

(9:32): "They wish to extinguish the Light of God, blowing with their mouths, while God will not allow that, for He will make His Light perfect, even if the unbelievers dislike it."

The unbelievers would like to blow out God's Light as it is a cause of offence to them. False teachers and preachers distort the Message of God by the false words of their mouth. Their wish is to put out the light of Truth for they are people of darkness; but God will perfect His Light, i.e., make it shine all the brighter in the eyes of people. His Light, in itself, is ever perfect but it will penetrate the hearts of people more and more and so become more and more perfect for them.

And in Verse 8:36, He gives a stark warning to the unbelievers who abuse the gifts and the wealth He bestowed on them:

(8:36): "Surely the unbelievers (those who deny the Truth) spend their wealth to hinder people from the Way of God. They will continue to so spend until their efforts become a source of intense regret for them, and then they will be vanquished, and then these unbelievers (deniers of the Truth) will be driven to Hell."

We don't want to be a complacent people, we want to be a people who love God and all His creatures with all our heart, soul, mind and strength. We must always remember that this life is a fleeting one, and the Hour of Judgment will be established and the Hereafter will commence.

Unfortunately, those who didn't believe in the Hereafter failed to realise that every action we take in this life inevitably leads to a consequence, whether it's positive or negative, unless God intervenes to save us from ourselves!

Let me remind you of popular Bible Verses from the Book of Zephaniah, who was sent as a Prophet to the Children of Israel:

"The LORD's anger will be like a fire that will burn up the whole world; suddenly He will bring an end, yes, an end to everyone on earth." "The LORD's day of judging is coming soon; it is near and coming fast."

Please don't ignore the obvious warnings. Don't neglect the teachings of the Torah and become secular.

God says in Verse
(62:5): "The example of those who were entrusted with the Torah and then did not take it on is like that of a donkey who carries volumes [of books]. Wretched is the example of the people who deny the signs of God. And God does not guide the wrongdoing people."

Regrettably, numerous Muslims, Christians, and Jews have disregarded the teachings of the Qur'an, the Bible, and the Torah, resulting in them becoming mere figures carrying books on their backs, akin to donkeys.

We should always reflect on God's declaration of **The Universal Brotherhood of Mankind**, mentioned in the Qur'an.

God says in Verse
(4:1): "O people! Fear your Lord Who created you from a single being (Adam) and out of it created its mate (Eve); and out of the two spread (like seeds) countless men and women. And fear God through whom you demand (your rights) from one another, and (do not sever) the ties of kinship. Surely God is ever watchful over you."

And He says in Verse
(30:22): "And among His Signs is the creation of the heavens and the earth, and the variations in your languages and your colours. Verily in that are Signs for those who know."

All mankind were created from a single pair of parents; yet they have spread to different countries and climates and developed different languages and different shades of complexions. And yet their basic unity remains unaltered. They feel in the same way and are all equally under God's care.

God reminds us in Verse 49:13, of this brotherhood, *"O mankind! We created you from a single (pair) of a male and female, and made you into nations and tribes that you may get to know each other (not to despise each other). Verily the most honoured of you in the sight of*

God is (he who is) the most righteous of you. Surely God has full knowledge and is well acquainted (with all things)."

This is addressed to all mankind and not only to the Muslim brotherhood. As it is, mankind is descended from one pair of parents. Their tribes, races and nations are convenient labels by which we may know certain differing characteristics. Before God they are all one, and the most honourable are the ones whom are most righteous.

May I remind you, my dear Jewish brothers and sisters, of the fate of the Syrian tyrant, Al-Assad (The Lion), who fled his country on 8th December 2024, after all his supporters and allies deserted him. Where was Russia or Iran or Hezbullah? He ran away like a little mouse, and he ended up in a Moscow Zoo.

On 14th January 2025, Israeli historian Ilan Pappe told Al Jazeera that he believes Zionism is entering its "last phase".

In his interview he said:

"I'm willing to say with some caution that this is the last phase of Zionism. Historically, such development in ideological movements, whether they are colonials or empires, doesn't matter, in the past, it's usually the final chapter, the ruthless one, the most ambitious one. And then it's too much and then they fall and collapse.

"When we say neo-Zionist, we mean, I think, that the old values of Zionism are now being more extreme, in a far more aggressive form than they were before, trying to

achieve in a short time what the previous generation of Zionists were trying to achieve in much longer, more incremental, gradual way.

"This is an attempt by a new leadership of Zionism to complete the work, if you want, that they started in 1948, namely of taking over officially the whole of historical Palestine and getting rid of as many Palestinians as possible.

"A scenario in which you have minimal American involvement is a positive scenario. The whole political structure that was built after the First World War is collapsing in front of our eyes and it includes Israel and Palestine.

"So, these are long regional processes which I think will benefit the Palestinians in the long run and will hopefully create a decolonised the country in the end. This is the product of a very indoctrinated society, from the cradle to the grave. They can see dead Palestinian babies and say, 'Good, very good'. This dehumanisation is part of the Israeli DNA and is very hard to confront just by giving them more information. There needs to be a fundamental reprogramming, so to speak."

I am deeply grateful to my very courageous, honest, and faithful Jewish brothers and sisters from the Board of Deputies of British Jews for their open letter dated 16th April 2025, to the Financial Times, which condemns the war in Gaza.

They warned that "Israel's soul is being ripped out". They said they could not "turn a blind eye or remain silent at this renewed loss of life and livelihoods". They also condemned violence against Palestinians in the occupied West Bank, which they said was encouraged by Prime Minister Benjamin Netanyahu's far-right administration, while warning: "This extremism also targets Israeli democracy.

"Israel's soul is being ripped out and we, members of the Board of Deputies of British Jews, fear for the future of the Israel we love and have such close ties to. Silence is seen as support for policies and actions that run contrary to our Jewish values," the letter said.

I can't simply finish the book before expressing my sincere gratitude to the French President Emmanuel Macron for announcing plans to recognise a Palestinian state, which could be implemented as early as June 2025.

Macron expressed his hope that by co-hosting a conference in June 2025 with Saudi Arabia, France is pushing for a two-state solution, that attendees who do not formally recognise Israel will, in turn, do so.

"We must move toward recognition, and we will do so in the coming months," said the French president. *"I'm not doing it for unity, or to please this or that person. I'm doing it because at some point it will be fair,"* he said.

France has always been in favour of a two-state solution but has resisted calls to recognise a Palestinian state, often arguing that Paris would only do so if it served the peace process.

Macron's comments came at the end of a three-day trip to Egypt, during which he visited a hospital treating Palestinians in the city of El Arish, near the border with Gaza, on 8th April 2025.

"I want to believe in peace; today the conflict has intensified and it's terrible … Since March 2, there's nothing going in [to the Gaza Strip] — no water, no food, no medication, and none of the injured are coming out," Macron said.

Out of love and sympathy for you, my dear Jewish brothers and sisters, I would like to share with you a story of Divine Warning and Human Arrogance, as narrated by God in verses 40:21-46.

In times long past, many powerful nations walked the earth—mighty in strength and renowned for the grand traces they left behind. Yet, despite their might, none could escape the reckoning of God. Their cities crumbled, their monuments became ruins, and their legacies faded—all because they rejected the messengers sent to them with clear signs of truth.

Among those warned were the Egyptians in the time of Prophet Moses. God had already sent Joseph to them centuries earlier, a foreigner turned savior who guided Egypt through famine and prosperity. Though they benefited materially, they dismissed his spiritual message, and after his death, arrogantly declared that no prophet would ever follow him. This denial sealed their hearts to future truth.

Then came Moses, armed with divine signs and a clear authority. But Pharaoh, his minister Haman, and the wealthy Qarun accused him of sorcery and falsehood. They were the embodiment of disbelief - Pharaoh, cruel and proud; Haman, the sycophantic courtier; and Qarun, the greedy and arrogant rich man. Together, they conspired not only to reject Moses but to kill the male children of the Israelites, fearing that one among them - perhaps Moses - might threaten their rule.

When Moses declared his faith and called upon the One God, Pharaoh plotted to kill him. Yet Moses stood firm, seeking refuge in the Lord of all, warning Pharaoh and his people of the Day of Account.

Amidst this tyranny, a lone believer from Pharaoh's own family stepped forward. He had hidden his faith, but now he spoke out: "Do you kill a man for saying, 'My Lord is God' - especially when he brings you clear proofs? If he lies, he bears the consequence. But if he speaks the truth, you will suffer for rejecting him. Who can protect us from God's wrath if it descends?"

He reminded them of the fates of past nations—Noah, 'Aad, Thamud—and how their rejection of divine truth led to ruin. "This life is fleeting," he said, "but the Hereafter is eternal. Those who act justly and believe will enter Paradise. But you invite me to disbelief and Hell, while I call you to salvation and forgiveness."

Despite his wisdom, Pharaoh's arrogance grew. He mocked Moses and ordered a tower to be built so he could ascend and see Moses' God, thinking to expose him as a liar. But this mockery sealed his fate. Evil became attractive in Pharaoh's eyes, and his delusions led him and his followers to ruin.

The Egyptian believer, placing his trust in God, was saved from their plots. But the people of Pharaoh were enveloped in torment—first in this life and, as the final blow, in the next. Morning and evening they are exposed to the Fire. And when Judgment Day comes, they will be cast into the severest punishment.

My dear Jewish brothers and sisters, I speak to you not as an enemy, but as the Egyptian man who once stood alone in Pharaoh's court—believing in Moses, pleading for the salvation of his people before it was too late. He tried to warn them. He urged them to turn back before wrath descended. But they were blinded by arrogance, deceived by power, and deaf to truth. Their strength could not save them.

And so I speak now to you, my dear Jewish brothers and sisters.

Despite the unmatched strength of your army, despite the precision of your intelligence services and the backing of the world's most powerful nations, they could not shield you from the horrors of October 7th. For over 20 months, you fought tirelessly against HAMAS, yet still, you could not claim total victory. What you face is not a religious war—it is a war over land, over rights, over dignity. And wars of this kind cannot be won by might alone.

There is a path forward. Not one of destruction, but of peace—through the only just solution left: two states, side by side, sharing the land that belongs to God, not to us.

Remember the words of Moses as recorded in the Qur'an (7:128): "

(7:128): "Seek help from God and be patient. Indeed, the earth belongs to God. He bestows it upon whom He pleases of His servants. And the favorable outcome is for the righteous."

Today, you hold power over the land—just as Pharaoh once held power over Moses and the Israelites. But power without righteousness invites downfall. Military might, alliances, and wealth cannot shield anyone from divine justice if it is provoked.

So I urge you: do not be like Pharaoh, who drowned in his own pride. Do not be like Goliath, who fell despite his strength. Be like Moses—who stood for justice. Be like David—who overcame tyranny with faith.

And remember: *"Among the people of Moses is a community which guides by truth and by it establishes justice." (7:159)*

Let that be you.

Before the pages of history turn once again—choose justice. Choose humility. Choose peace. For in the end, it is not who holds the land, but who holds to the truth, that will prevail.

Bibliography

A) Qur'anic Sources, Translations, Tafasir, Etc.

Ali, Abdullah Yusuf. *The Meaning of The Holy Qur'an*, Beltsville, Maryland: Amana Publications, 2001.

Al-Ghazaly, Mohammed. *Nahwa Tafsir Mawdo'ee Le-Sewar Al-Qur'an Al-Karim.* Cairo, Egypt: Dar Ash-Shorouq, 1st Edition, 1995.

Al-Mahalli, Jalal Al-Din and Al-Suyuti, Jalal Al-Din. *Tafsir Al-Imamain Al-Jalalayn.* Beirut, Lebanon: 1974.

Al-Nasafi, Abdullah Ibn Ahmad. *Tafsir Al-Qur'an Al-Jalil.* Cairo, Egypt: Al-America Press, 1936.

Al-Sha'rawi, Mohammed Metwalli. *Tafsir Al-Sha'rawi.* Cairo, Egypt: Akhbar El-Yom Press, 1975.

Barlas, Asma. *Believing Women in Islam: Unreading Patriachal Interpretations of the Qur'an.* Austin, USA: University of Texas Press, 2002.

Ibn-Kathir, Emaduldin Ismail. *Tafsir Al-Qur'an Al-Azim.* Cairo, Egypt: Dar Ehiaulkutub Al-Arabia, Esa Al-Baby Al-Halaby Press, 1946.

Ismael, Mohammed Bakr. *Kholasat At-Tafsir.* Cairo, Egypt: Dar Almanar, 1995.

Kassam, Zayn. *The Hermeneutics of Problematic Gender Verses in the Qur'an.* London and New Jersey: Zed Books, 1996.

Tantawy, Moammed Said. *Banu-Israel fi Al-Qur'an wa As-Sunna.* Cairo, Egypt: Dar Ash-Shorouk, 2nd Edition, 2000.

Wadud-Muhsin, Amina. *Qur'an and Woman,* Kuala Lumpar: Penerbit Fajar Bakti Sdn.Bhd, 1994.

B) Fatwas Sources

Al-Qaradawi, Yusuf. *Fatawi Mu'aasera* Cairo, Egypt: Dar Al- Qalam, 6th Edition, 1996.

Ibn-Taimeia, Abi-Alabbas Taqi Al-Din Ahmad Ibn Abdul-Halim. *Al-Fatawi Al-Kubra.* Beirut, Lebanon: Dar Al-M'arefa,

Saqr, Ateya. *Al-Fatawi.* Cairo, Egypt: Al-Maktaba Al-Tawfeqeia

C) Fiqh Sources

Abu-Zohra, Mohammed. *Osool Al-Fiqh.* Cairo, Egypt: Dar Al-Fikr Al-Araby, 1997.

Al-Gazery, Abdul-Rahman. *The Book of Fiqh as per the Four Mazhabs.* Cairo, Egypt: Dar Al-Irshad,

Al-Ghazaly, Mohammed. *Fiqh As-Serah.* Alexandria, Egypt: Dar Al-D'awa 6th Edition, 2000.

314

Al-Ghazaly, Mohammed. *As-Sunnah An-Nabawia bain Ahl Al-Fiqh wa Ahl Al-Hadith.* Cairo, Egypt: Dar Ash-Shorouk, 2011.

Al-Qaradawi, Yusuf. *Fiqh Al-Awlaweyat.* Cairo, Egypt: Maktabet Wahba, 3rd Edition, 1999.

Al-Qaradawi, Yusuf. *The Lawful and the Prohibited in Islam.* Plainfield, Indiana, USA: American Trust Publications, 1994.

Al-Sha'rawi, Mohammed Metwalli. *Al-Fiqh Al-Islami, 100 Questions and Answers.* Cairo, Egypt: Maktabat At-Turath Al-Islami,

Darwesh, Hussain Ali. *Al-Merath fi Al-Islam as per the Four Mazhabs* Cairo, Egypt: Al-Zahra Lel-Ilam Al-Araby, 5th Edition, 1987.

Ibn-Hazm, Abi Mohammed Ali Bin-Ahmad Bin-Said. *Al-Muhalla*, Cairo, Egypt: Dar Al-Turath,
Ismael, Dr Mohammed Bakr. *Al-Fiqh Al-Wadheh mena Al-Ketab wa Assuna based on the Four Mazhabs*, Cairo, Egypt: Dar Al-Manar, 1990.
Sabeq, As'sayed. *Fiqh As'sunnah*. Beirut, Lebanon: Dar Al-Ketab Al-Araby & Cairo, Egypt: Dar Al-Fath, 2004.

D) Scientific Sources
Board of Researchers under the Research Programme of 1985-1990, *Scientific Indications in the Holy Qur'an*, Dhaka, Bangladesh: Islamic Foundation Bangladesh, 2nd Edition, 1995.
Bucaille, Maurice. *What is the Origin of Man?* Urdu Nagar, LHR: Al-Falah Islamic Books, 5th Edition, 1989.

E) Other Islamic Sources
Abdel Haleem, Harfiyah; Ramsbotham, Oliver; Risaluddin, Saba and Wicker, Brian. *The Crescent and the Cross, Muslim and Christian Approach to War and Peace*, Great Britain: MacMillan Press Ltd, 1998.
Abu Shuqqa, Abdul Halim Mohammed. *Tahreer Al-Maraa fi Asr Ar-Resalah*. Cairo, Egypt & Kuwait: Dar Al-Qalam, 8th Edition, 2010.
Ad-Dhahabi, Muhammad Bin Uthman. *The Chief Sins (Al-Kaba'r)*. Beirut, Lebanon: Dar Al-Kotob Al-Ilmiyah, 1st Edition, 1999.
Al-Ghazaly, Mohammed. *Kholoq Al-Muslim*. Cairo, Egypt: Dar Nahdet Misr, 22nd Edition, 2014.
An-Nawawi, Abu Zakariya Yahya Bin Sharaf. *Riyadh-us-Saleheen*. Karachi, Pakistan: Dar Ahy'a us-Sunna Al-Nabawiy'a, 1984.

Engineer, Asghar Ali. *The Rights of Women in Islam.* USA.UK.INDIA: New Dawn Press, Inc., 2nd Revised Edition, 2004.

Printed in Dunstable, United Kingdom